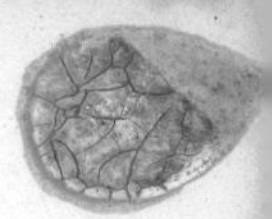

AF594086

Dear Sir, Drop Dead!

EDITED BY *DONALD CARROLL*

DEAR SIR, DROP DEAD!

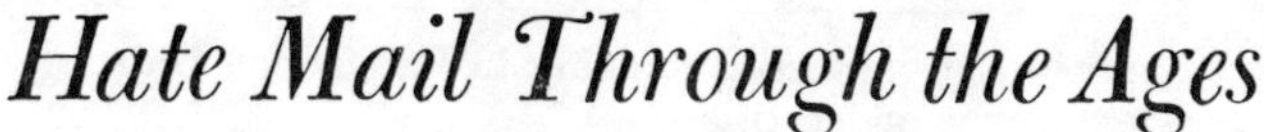

Hate Mail Through the Ages

COLLIER BOOKS
A Division of Macmillan Publishing Co., Inc.
NEW YORK

Copyright © 1979 by Carroll Regnier Associates

All rights reserved. No part of this book may be reproduced or transmitted in any form or by any means, electronic or mechanical, including photocopying, recording or by any information storage and retrieval system, without permission in writing from the Publisher.

Macmillan Publishing Co., Inc.
866 Third Avenue, New York, N.Y. 10022
Collier Macmillan Canada, Ltd.

Library of Congress Cataloging in Publication Data
Main entry under title:

Dear sir, drop dead!

1. Hate mail. I. Carroll, Donald, 1940-
PN6140.H38D4 826'.008'0353 79-4681
ISBN 0-02-040360-7

First Printing 1979

Printed in the United States of America

FOR

KANKO

AND

HEINER

The symbol of the human race ought to be an ax;
every human being has one concealed about
him somewhere.

—MARK TWAIN

Acknowledgments

To Alfred A. Knopf, Inc. for permission to use the two letters from *Letters of H.L. Mencken*, by H.L. Mencken, edited by Guy J. Forgue. Copyright © 1961 by Alfred A. Knopf, Inc. Reprinted by permission of Alfred A. Knopf, Inc.

To Michigan State University Press for permission to reprint the letter by Frederick William Rolfe from *The Quest for Corvo*, by A.J. Symons.

To Viking Penguin Inc. for permission to reprint the three letters by Alexander Woollcott.

To the Trustees of the Estate of Clara Clemens Samassoud for permission to reprint the three letters by Mark Twain.

To Max Wilk, author of *The Wit and Wisdom of Hollywood*, for permission to reprint the telegram by Will Rogers.

To the Society of Authors on behalf of the Bernard Shaw Estate for permission to reprint the letter by George Bernard Shaw.

To all the wonderful but occasionally misunderstood people who opened their smoldering mailboxes for the benefit of this book, with special thanks to Elkan Allan, Colman Andrews, Prof. Fredrica Bartz, Charles Berlitz, Erma Bombeck, William F. Buckley, Jr., Tim Cahill, Jon Carroll, Craig Claiborne, Peggy Dakyns, Anthony Haden-Guest, Al Heitzer, Terry Helbing, Warren Hinckle, Philip J. Klass, Dick Lochte, George Melly, Richard Meltzer, Jessica

Mitford, Edwin Newman, Rep. David R. Obey, Madalyn Murray O'Hair, Virginia Peterson, John Simon, Dwayne Tinsley, Dr. Zev Wanderer, Lord Willis, and Senator Stephen M. Young.

To L. Patrick Coyle, whose diligence and resourcefulness was of incalculable help with the historical research.

Contents

Introduction: The Mailed Fist

If there were ever any doubts about the shrewdness of George Wallace's political judgment, they were dispelled forever when the governor chose as his campaign slogan: SEND THEM A MESSAGE. As public exhortations go, that must surely rank among the most irresistible of all time.

It is not difficult to see why. Ever since the invention of the alphabet, one of the great—and for some people, one of the few—pleasures in life has been to send Them a message, one that calls attention to major defects in Themselves. Traditionally these messages have been transmitted by letter, hence the unattractive term invented by Them to refer to—and dismiss—such communications: "hate mail."

The fact is, however, that the term "hate mail,"

though it has come to enjoy wide currency, scarcely does justice to what is probably the most popular and enduring genre of folk literature in the world. Certainly it is the most colorful. It is also unique in at least one respect: it is the only literary form that has always had more practitioners than readers. This is partly due to the fact that certain people attract a disproportionate number of correspondents; but it's also because the more inspired writers, in the exaltation of their *furor scribendi*, sometimes ignore such boring details as getting the address right.

This imbalance in the ratio of writers to readers is to be deplored, for it means that, by and large, the world has been deprived of the opportunity to savor some of the most memorable and unorthodox literary creations ever composed. And it is not a little surprising, given the legions of underemployed scholars and critics who, one would have thought, should be transported into ecstasy by the chance to practice their exegetical skills on such a voluptuous body of virgin material. Yet it has been consistently, shamefully neglected.

Why should this be so? The principal reason, of course, is that most people have the unfortunate but understandable tendency to throw away hate mail as soon as it arrives, consequently there is not much of it available for inspection. Abusive letters are an acquired taste, and, like rocks that arrive through the window, they make difficult-to-explain souvenirs. But there are other reasons, many others, why hate-mail collecting is not yet as popular as, say, stamp collecting, as I have learned in the course of putting together this book.

To begin with, there is the fear on the part of the addressees that others might take seriously—or worse, might agree with—some of the less flattering sentiments expressed in such letters. Howard Cosell, for example, feels that publication of the unfriendly greetings that he has received from time to time would be bad for his "image." (One will perhaps be forgiven for wondering how anything could be bad for Mr. Cosell's image.) And Johnny Carson, while admitting that he keeps all of his hate mail, has decided that he would, on the whole, be more comfortable if it remained exclusively in his custody.

Others have aesthetic objections to seeing their hate mail in print. Brigid Brophy, the English author, claims sadly that her correspondents display "a turn for sheer rather than witty abuse," a lament echoed by Jean Rook, the popular columnist for the London *Daily Express*: "The many people who loathe me seem to be neither clever nor witty, just bloody rude." Therefore, she adds, she has no "deep green interesting poison" to share with others.

Arnold Schwarzenegger, on the other hand, takes a moral position regarding the publication of hate mail. "I do not want this kind of letter published," he says, flexing his mind, because "I do not write nasty letters to people and feel that this should not be encouraged." Shame on me.

Another factor contributing to the scarcity of hate mail in print is that, strange as it may seem, many apparently truthful people claim never to have received any. Don Meredith, for one, insists that his mail "is all very nice." Colin Reid, of the London *Daily Mail*, goes even further: "Everybody writes to say how lovely I am."

The controversial sculptor Carl Andre reports that "people seem inclined to attack me in person" rather than in correspondence, while Quentin Crisp, the flamboyant English homosexual whose autobiography, *The Naked Civil Servant*, was dramatized on television a couple of years ago, says that being listed in the London telephone directory prevents him from receiving any truly interesting mail. In economically hard-pressed Britain, Mr. Crisp's antagonists economize by phoning in their outrage.

Barbara Walters is another one who sees no evil. Indeed, for Miss Walters there is no such thing as hate mail. There *is* the occasional "derogatory" mail from people she calls her "fans"—but this exceptional type of fan mail, one gathers, is hastily fed into the incinerator.

And then there is Senator Thomas Eagleton of Missouri. Senator Eagleton, who, it will be remembered, was rather cruelly jettisoned by George McGovern in 1972 after reports were published raising questions about his mental health, seemed to have considerable difficulty in understanding my letter requesting permission to look at his hate mail. He replied that the "demands" on him were so great as to prevent him from complying with my "request for the completion of a questionnaire." The demands on the senator are clearly not only great but unusual.

However, Senator Eagleton is by no means alone in

being confused by a straightforward request to see hate mail. In fact, while I was compiling this collection it occurred to me that Senator McGovern may have committed a grievous error in removing Eagleton as his running mate. There is manifestly a sizable constituency in the country for Eagleton's way of thinking.

This lugubrious realization came after publication of a small advertisement that I placed in a number of national magazines. The advertisement was inserted on the assumption that few people can have lived lives so drearily unprovocative as to be untouched by people writing in tongues. It invited readers to send in any nasty, funny letters they had received. The response was enormous.

Alas.

Out of the deluge of mail that poured in, there was only one letter from a reader who obviously knew exactly what I was looking for. It was from a gentleman incarcerated in Attica prison for a crime of violence. Among the other letters I received—apart from those addressed to "Advertising Manager, Hate Mail," sent by eager space sellers for other magazines—the most prominent category consisted of rebukes for placing the advertisement at all, "when what the world needs now is love not hate."

At the same time, there were large numbers of people who felt that the world could profit from a little hate—theirs. As a result, I quickly found myself ankle-deep in fuzzy carbon copies of letters that had supposedly reduced to rubble all manner of predatory landlords, neighbors, dentists, shopkeepers, in-laws, and others put here to test us. These were written by people who had probably been taught that the pen is mightier than the sword. Sad to say, in every case the writer would have been better served by a sword.

The same holds true, almost, for the various Hollywood gag-writers who urged upon me examples of their drollery, accompanied by brisk enquiries as to how many cute hate letters I would like. These people, I concluded, would be better served by a razor blade, possibly applied in a bathtub filled with warm water.

Which brings me to the First Law Concerning Hate Mail. It is as follows: Unless one happens to be unnaturally gifted, it is impossible to sit down and manufacture, with a wicked grin and some carbon paper, an authentic hate letter. Authentic hate letters come from the heart, or at least from something similarly muscular and driven.

While this principle was understood, if only intuitively, by most of the people who answered my advertisement, there were other, even more elemental distinctions made in the advertisement which proved to be beyond the grasp of many readers.

There was a letter from a lady in Colorado, helpfully headed "HATE LETTER," in which she complained bitterly to me that her husband always came home drunk at night—but in the last paragraph she took it all back, confiding that they could probably work things out. A gentleman in Trinidad sent a poem entitled "My Wife Expects Too Much of Me" (sample lines: *I find / That I am in a decadence of mind / And that marriage is very hard / At this point . . .*). And a sidewalk *philosophe* in Vancouver favored me with an interminable discourse which began: "This is what I hate: the mind of man. Not *my* mind specifically or *your* mind. . . ." Someday I must finish the letter.

A young lady in Boston sent in a whole sheaf of intimate letters from her former lover. She regarded these as hate mail because now she hated him. An army private stationed in California forwarded a letter from his girl friend in which she explained, quite gently, why she did not wish to see him again. His reason for considering it hate mail: "It contains six lies!"

A gentleman in New York City was pleased to let me have a representative sampling of the voluminous correspondence he had directed at book publishers. "For some years past," he explained, "I have held the copyright on the word *the*. . . ."—and not surprisingly, he had detected what can only be described as promiscuous violations of his copyright, causing him to notify publishers, angrily and at length, of the precise extent of their trespass on his property. He is, if it's any consolation to the publishing industry, behind in his work.

Another New Yorker wrote enclosing a letter he had sent to the *New York Times*. The letter began, promisingly enough, "It's an outrage!" But it steadily lost momentum as the nature of the outrage slowly emerged: the *Times* had, in the opinion of the correspondent, deliberately put a false clue in one of its crossword puzzles. Still, the letter might have been usable if it had closed with a strong rhetorical flourish. Instead, it ended with a sheepish P.S. in which the writer, having suddenly deciphered the tainted clue, admitted that he had been wrong all along.

Most mysterious of all, a number of people were moved to reply to the advertisement by clipping it out and sending it back to me unencumbered by a covering letter. My initial reaction was to assume, gratefully, that the remaining surrealists and minimalists among us had made common cause. Then I was stricken by the paralyzing suspicion that my correspondents were trying to be funny. This, I'm afraid, was probably the case: a second glance at the typeface in which the advertisements were set revealed that they were all sent in by readers of *Psychology Today.*

In addition to the letters that disqualified themselves, there were many that I was obliged to exclude because, however splendidly hateful they were, they failed to meet the criteria I laid down when I embarked on this project. Thus, for example, there are no letters here from the professionals, those congenitally cranky souls whose only known purpose in life is to spread their contempt evenly and indiscriminately over mankind. It is not, I hasten to add, their misanthropy that has caused their banishment from this volume but their tendency to deploy their resources too thinly. To properly appreciate the work of each, one must study the entire *oeuvre.*

Nonetheless, I would be remiss if I did not pay homage to some of these dedicated men and women. Foremost among them, by common consent of his victims, is the legendary George Richards of Poole, Dorset, in England. Unfortunately, Mr. Richards's typewriter fell silent a few years ago, but for decades he was the scourge of every editor, columnist, reviewer, commentator, broadcaster, and public personality in England. To judge by his formidable output, no utterance was too mumbled, no print too small, to escape his attention if it contained an attitude or opinion that he deemed punishable by letter (which would, more often than not, open with the heartwarming salutation, "Pitiable Imbecile: . . ."). In his declining years, perhaps sensing that his powers of vituperation were failing him, he resorted to sending his enemies toilet seats—C.O.D.

The torch so marvelously kept aflame by Mr. Richards has now been passed to Mrs. Peggy Dakyns of London, a nice lady whose grandmotherly charm belies her true calling. In recent months Mrs. Dakyns has written letters attacking programs designed to help the elderly ("the 'good neighbor' campaigns whereby they come in at any hour to see how we are keeping ourselves warm"), retirement homes ("Is there also a resident undertaker prepared to take measurements at short notice?"), Alex Comfort ("who betrays his own sex . . . older women can also have their pick of much younger men"), Andy Warhol (who appeals only to "moronic voyeurs"), *The Sound of Music* (which is loaded with "sinister" appeal due to its "wrapped-up sex with a vengeance"), critics (who are "pathetic . . . they are all phoneys"), Englishmen ("I have never in my life met one who could even loosely be described as a gentleman. This might explain their spectacular failure with women . . ."), and men in general ("I consider the male sex a very short-term investment because not only do they not wear as well as women, they die much quicker —though I am not complaining. . . .").

Lastly, in this context, one should mention Dr. Jesse Bryant, a New York City psychiatrist. For sheer stamina, Dr. Bryant stands alone among contemporary letter-writers. Dr. Bryant's specialty is grumpy letters to the editor. No one, including Dr. Bryant, knows for certain how many of them he has written, but over the past six years alone 274 of them have been published in New York newspapers.

Also omitted from this collection are letters from whiners. The whiners, a long-faced and populous tribe, generally inhabit the outskirts of one's consciousness, where as far as one can tell, their days are mostly spent being, in turn, rudely awakened, somewhat disturbed, mildly shocked, not amused, quite distressed, rather perturbed, sadly disillusioned, greatly disappointed, and, in the final analysis, worried about the consequences.

Nor are there any genuinely threatening letters. Mental derangement is amusing only up to a point. Perhaps the most bizarre illustration of the point at which looniness ceases to be funny was a letter written several years ago to Tim Cahill of *Rolling Stone*. Cahill had written an article in which he suggested that Mark Spitz, while wondrous to behold in the water, was not perhaps the brightest of men. Whereupon a letter arrived accusing Cahill of saying naughty things about the greatest swimmer of all time and warning him that God was going to kill him for his impertinence. Cahill chuckled and pinned the letter up on his bulletin board. Shortly thereafter Cahill discovered that the gentleman who wrote the letter, now a resident of San Quentin, had been quite busy on the day that he sent his warning: he had also found the time to go to Mill Valley, near San Francisco, and murder an entire family. The letter is no longer on Cahill's bulletin board.

Another type of letter-writer not represented here is the smiling saboteur who relies on the soft bank shot to do his dirty work. Alexander Woollcott was a master of this technique. On one occasion, when a lady asked him to help her daughter get into a private school by writing a letter of recommendation, Woollcott wrote—or pretended that he wrote—to the school's headmistress imploring her to accept "this unfortunate child" and thereby remove her from her shocking environment, where she was being subjected to the most unspeakable influences, what with the nightly orgies and all.

Along the same lines, there is the case of Judge William H. Underwood, an eccentric nineteenth-century Georgian who was asked by his ambitious son to write a letter of introduction for him to the governor of Georgia. The judge readily acceded to his son's request, and a few weeks later the young Underwood proudly presented the governor with a sealed message which, when opened, read: "This will be handed you by my son John. He has the greatest thirst for an office, with the least capacity to fill one, of any boy you ever saw."

I have also decided, with some regret, that printed dunning letters do not belong in an anthology such as this. This means that the reader will not find here—or, one hopes, anywhere at home—that delightful missive from the U.S. Internal Revenue Service which carries the heading, "FINAL NOTICE BEFORE SEIZURE." (This is possibly the most poignant use of language in the limited repertoire of the American bureaucracy, for recipients of the notice frequently do have a seizure before they have a chance to read anybody else's notice.)

Only marginally less intimidating is the demand sent out by the collection agencies belonging to the Associated Credit Bureaus of America. There are 3,600 of them, as they like to remind folks, and they take a collectively dim view of deadbeats and others who demonstrate a cavalier attitude toward the payment of bills. So what they do is send out notices which—in addition to the standard typographical bullying: lots of red ink and capital letters and exclamation marks—carry an outline map of the United States splattered with dots to show how ubiquitous they are. Underneath the map, for the benefit of those who may be slow in getting the message, there is the flinty-eyed boast: "Distance Means Nothing to Us."

And there are those letters which are not in themselves very hateful or amusing, but which carry rather startling addresses. Ezra Pound, for instance, used to send tedious broadsides addressed to the *Ladies' Home Urinal.* And Stephen Birnbaum, the travel editor of *Esquire*, not long ago received a letter addressed simply to "Jerk." Mr. Birnbaum was less disturbed by the letter than by the assumption on the part of his colleagues that the envelope was meant for him.

I should mention that within this particular species of letter there is a large and growing subspecies: letters written and addressed by computers. These, of course, are only accidentally offensive, but the offense they give can often be intense indeed. There is the recent example of the Chicago systems analyst (or "SYS ANAL" in the vocabulary of the computer) who received a letter from Time, Inc., addressed to "Mr. Anal." He was not amused. Nor was Irwin George of Tulsa, Oklahoma, when the computer at a Connecticut mail-order firm insisted on addressing the company's catalogues and bills to "Idiot George."

Additionally, and for reasons that I hope are obvious, it has not been possible to include nonverbal communications in this collection. Which is a pity, because they sometimes make their points most graphically. Anita Bryant can attest to this. In the course of her crusade against homosexuality Miss Bryant has received numerous photographs depicting two or more gentlemen enjoying one another's company in ways displeasing to her. There is, too, the business tycoon in London whose disinclination to waste time waiting for tardy luncheon guests to show up has prompted him more than once to retreat into his office and pour the lunches into Jiffy bags, which are then mailed to the wretched latecomers.

Finally, and again with a reluctance, I have ruled out posthumous hate mail: accusatory suicide notes, vindictive wills, that sort of thing. Although one should note in passing a wonderful epitaph seen on a tombstone in Tennessee: I TOLD YOU I WAS SICK.

This elaborate winnowing process, though it imposed upon me the painful necessity of rejecting some quite remarkable expressions of disgust, was for the worthy purpose of enabling me, without distraction, to assemble the real classics in the annals of poison-penmanship. As a consequence, it is my belief that the letters gathered here conform, each in its own way, to the highest standards of inventive invective.

Some of the letters were written by old masters, others were composed by stylists of the epistolary avant-garde. Some will delight only the connoisseur, others will appeal mainly to those who have just begun to discover the lyricism of nastiness. But whatever the taste to which the individual letters may appeal, they should all, taken together, satisfy a deep hunger shared by every one of us: that profound and very human craving to read other people's mail.

I

Letters to Television Performers and Network Executives

To William F. Buckley, Jr., host of the television program "Firing Line"

You make me sick! I've never heard a person I'd like to shut up as much as I would you. If you saw yourself, as many do, your leer, sneer and malicious grin, if you had any sense, you'd take yourself off TV.

Didn't your nanny tell you as a child not to interrupt someone that is talking? Do you ever listen? Do you ever let anyone finish a statement without pushing your obnoxious self in? You are really a perfect example of a spoiled creature of the rich and inbred.

If it wasn't for the great guests you have, for sure you wouldn't have a program. If you would listen more to people like Ellsberg, Galbraith, etc., you could learn a lot and be of greater service and utilize your time on TV for better things.

Take some of your excess money and buy yourself a TV station.

(EDITOR'S NOTE: Mr. Buckley replied, "I've done that. What shall I do next?")

To Edwin Newman, television news commentator

Saw you today on TV. Never liked what you said and making such faces. Never again will I listen to you.

You are nothing but an ugly Big Mouth.

To Lord Willis, writer of the hugely successful British television series "Dixon of Dock Green," who has himself frequently appeared on television, on which occasions he has questioned the wisdom of paying heed to monarchists, deists, and racists

I was disgusted watching you on tele tonight twiddling your thumbs and calmly decrying YOUR Queen the authority over you. The beatles are rubbish I agree. MY PEOPLE ARE NOT RUBBISH no more than you are. You don't feel any loyalty to your own country and our Dear Queen. Why not resign your position on her bench?

Do not quote the Sermon on the Mount. It won't help you.

"Whoso looketh on a woman to lust after her hath commited adultery against her in his heart."

You are not so clever as you think.

One thing that strikes me about you and your type is

your appalling intolerance and bigotry. You cannot bear to hear an opposite view stated.

Atheists have their moments of doubt.

One night you may wake up in terror and realize that there is a God and that He has commanded laws which are to be obeyed and wrath to all who wilfully disobey.

Your state of hero-worshipping hysteria of the black man is a very grave symptom of a fell disease.

Consult a psychiatrist, pronto!! Otherwise you run the risk of being put out to grass with the donkeys.

You do not know anything about Coloured People. Live and work with them. Close your mouth on what you dont know about. It is people like you talk who are wrapped in cotton wool. Our daughter cannot go out after dark our houses are broken into our bags are pinched.

So shut your bloody mouth and talk about what you know about. If these blacks are caught by the police the judge pats them on the head and calls them good little wogs and lets them go. It is the White People who want protecting not the black. So shut your bloody mouth and talk about something you know about. *And thats not much.*

Dear *overrated* Lord Willis of Wog Green, Stuff *all* Immigrants on England's back, *and* their needs, wishes and desires. Send then *all* to Bloody Bogside, Tel-Aviv or Bangle-Desh. And take your useless self with them.

Perhaps out there you can start a new TV tripe series called "Abdul-Sean-O'Dinga-Moishe of Wog Green."

And take De Great White Scots Idiot Dr. Ramsey of Ganges with you. He most certainly will not be missed.

The real sickening set-up is YOU, an out and out Communist, accepting a peerage! What a hypocrite!

It is people like you who make this world the *rotten* place it is today.

To Madalyn Murray O'Hair, the prominent atheist and television polemicist, in acknowledgment of her long and intermittently successful labors to have acts of religious piety proscribed on public occasions and to have devotional phrases expunged from U.S. government documents and artifacts

Woman, I come against you in the name of the Lord God of Isreal.

I saw you and heard you on television. Who are you to try to defy the God of Heaven? I am acquainted with him. You'd better be.

On TV you looked like a big mouth devil. You are a devil possessed woman. What are you to criticize the

Astranauts, for reading the Word? You'd better read and believe it.

Some time you will die, as many people do. Woman you had better take down your sign.

Dear Mrs. O'Hair, You and your animal friends figure that God can't judge you but you know darn well that I can and you are shure going to feel my judgement. Any male who calls you or your friends women and men cannot be called a man.

This is not my full judgement but it will do for a start. Don't be too cocky about you and your friends having most of the money because God told me the solution to that problem.

Madalyn Murray O'Hair, She Devil—Mind your damn business. I hope that you lose your stupid brain. We are fed up with snakes. You are a low type of snake. Your husband is a just plain rat and the same to him! You are worse than Judas and so is your rat husband. If you was my mother you wouldn't live 24 hours. Please tell somebody to spit in your face for me.

May you be damned to hell with you!

Madalyn O'Hair, I cant understand why you dont think that there is a God when he send all this good Rain. Where do you think this bad weather come from?

Dear Heathen Communist Bitch: Words cannot express my Contempt for you. You should have your tongue cut out. The very idea of attempting to ban Prayer from space or any other place. Shame on you! Don't you dare come to Charleston or we will tear you limb from limb. People like you are what is wrong with this country today. You should be slowly burned at the state with no prayers allowed.

Mrs. O'Hair, I am going to give you a peice of my mind. What do you think you're doing? Why do you want to do that?

I think you should go to Russia, where there is no religion.

O'hair, I hope you loose every suit that you file, but you probably wont. The Devil takes care of his own. There is nothing wrong in Bingo people injoying playing. There is nothing wrong in playing poker so long as you dont cheat, and one does not deprive their families of what is needed.

Who are you people to speak of law and decency. If there is no God, then nothing is wrong. Laws are not needed. The animals know no God, therefore they have no laws and no decency. They dont care who sees them in a sexual act.

Madalyn O'Hair, You devilish character that is living in this wonderful FREE Nation, and you dare to degrade our Christian Faith.

I would suggest that you be shipped out of this country on a flight across the ocean into Russia where you belong and may they place you in prison or in a field camp with the bolshevicks and that they harrass you into insanity.

Dear God, c/o Madalyn Murray O'Hair:
Destroy the following cities in Texas:

Borger
Pampa
Amarillo
Wichita Falls
Denton
Fort Worth
Cleburne
Lubbock
Abilene
Sweetwater
Big Spring
El Paso
San Angelo
Del Rio
San Antonio
Victoria
Corpus Christi
Laredo
Sherman
Dallas
Longview
Marshall
½ Texarkana
Bryan
Beaumont
Houston
Galveston
Port Athur
Waco
Temple
Taylor

Thirty-one in all.

Dear Mrs. or *Mr.* O'Hair, I saw you on TV last night for the first time and that explained everything for me. Your large masculine business executive face with a 10 year old girl's hair style conveys a very mixed up individual and explains all your current thinkings and rantings. You are just lashing out at God in anger because you came off the assembly line ¾ masculine and ¼ feminine.

Katherine Murry O'Hare, Atheist Woman—Texas was a good place untill you came here. Why dont you go back where you came from. You and Judas go hang your self. On television you look like a she devil in the form of a human. Your own son probally hates you.

I heard you would not give out your address in Austin. You old coward.

Dear Satan II, I am only 14 but I believe in God and the Bible. If you don't believe in God or the Bible just keep it to yourself. Keep your Big Mouth Shut. There's more Christians in this world than people like you and I'm glad too! If you want to know I use silent prayer in my school all the time and I'd like to see you do something about that.

I think you should be tarred and feathered, stoned, and boiled in oil.

Madeline Murry O'Hair, You ugly Son of B! Also your ignorant son. Of what? Idiots.

Thank God that we have women like Anita O'Bryant

and Mrs. Schafley and 100 million others also. Decent all. Soon you will get your greeting to the Devil in Hell. Plus your idiot offspring.

Miss O'Hair, What are you some kind of a nut, that you don't want prayer. You are headed straight for Hell, unless you change your ways.

Miss O'Hare—You are the most hatefulest woman anybody has ever heard of. Why don't you just leave all of our Religions alone.

All you are is nothing but a big old witch with a big ugly fat face and mouth on you. You are also nothing but a big fat Atheist Freak.

We will worship the Lord any way we want to, I am speaking for all the Different Religions in the United States, as you cannot ban anything in this country, that even includes Christmas, Thanksgiving, Easter, and Physical Education in our schools, cause if we want Religion in our Homes, Schools, and Churches, besides Physical Education, we will have it. You keep your damn mouth out of our business so you might as well forget it.

Dear Devil O'Hair, Who do you think you are. One day there will be a day you will be sorry for what you done.

In your heart your fighting God.

You may stand on your Beliefs till you die. But one day you will bow at the feet of Christ who died for us on a tree.

Mrs. O'Hare, You must be possessed of the Devil. Your just too evil to live. If the Indians were still around they'd scalp the likes of you—and hang your WIG on a flagpole.

To the Atheist, Madeline O'Hair Murray—Did you ever see your horrible face on TV. If I were you I'd hide it with shame. I think your profession should be other than you contemplate and I really would enjoy seeing you behind bars (not animal cages for they are better in character than you) but in *jail.*

You big fat slob—and really I would like to write some of the rotten descriptions you fit under. Get wise to yourself—you are not dead yet—who do you think you are. Earn a legitimate living—or I hope you are eventually arrested.

Dear Mrs. "Shit-Ass" Murry-O'Hair: Why you *silly*, *ignorant*, *assinine* old woman! Your husband ought to smash you in the teeth every morning. It's a wonder someone hasn't already done it for him. Evidently you're a Communist! You must be in your dotage and age of senility to do what you're doing.

You're just a silly woman trouble maker who needs

a "head-shrinker." Doe-doe! You ought to be in the booby hatch and the key thrown away!

Ms. O'Hair, One of these days, millions of people suddenly are going to vanish without any warning! And *you*, Madalyn Murray O'Hair, are going to wonder why! It will be very soon—perhaps in the next 20 or 25 years.

To executives of the television networks

I just saw the previews for next weeks "Hawaii Five-O." There was a short display of Miss Universe contestants followed by this dialogue between two of your program stars:

"There was no evidence of violence or forcible entry. . . ."

Treating this as a laughing stock warrants pillorying.

If I see you on a day a rape has been perpetrated, I'll be prone to put unduly stress on your couldn't-give-a-shit face.

Last evening at 11:25 we heard your local newscaster say something about Boston. The next instant, he was describing a dead child's frozen hand in a mitten. My husband and I were sickened.

Already this week, we've had to watch 1,000 dolphins screaming on a beach while Walter Cronkite described the slaughter. My sons ran out of the room.

We didn't use to watch your news, but three months ago we started watching. No sooner had we switched, when they ran a news item showing police digging the frozen corpse of an elderly woman out of a snow bank.

This is the worst piece ever aired. We all get the message, believe me, when we hear the words, child discovered near own doorstep after blizzard. Something along that line would have been sufficient.

I recently pledged $5 per month to public television. It was with the understanding that Sesame Street was going to be on for 4 hrs. on Sunday. That was a deception from the start. Today, there was only one hour of SS, followed by some no talent and then whatever it was.

I therefore cancel my pledge. You won't be hearing from me again! The bait and switch has no business being on Public TV. Get the chronic college students and the Spanish population to fund these shows.

So someone being in JAIL is more important to you than someone who has undergone OPEN HEART SURGERY. Your program owes the Heart Surgeons more than 15 minutes. I speak from experience—6 years ago this month I had such an operation—the doctors saved my life—I had four heart attacks before this surgery. I hope YOU never have a heart attack and need by-pass surgery!

I'm tired of hearing about Rachel Tension. All she does is make trouble. It's about time you shut up talking about her.

What in hell is the matter with your news team in this town?

What was so damned amusing about the item concerning the lost mother-cat with the amputated tail? To the concerned owners there was nothing very hilarious about it.

The whole news team repeatedly smirks and grins even after a report of a tragic incident in the news.

Don't tell me they have an irrepressible sense of humor. So do little boys and girls in the third grade.

You do have some excellent programs, but "Tom Brown's School Days" has made me sick. My husband has read the book, and we have it right here. He tells me your program is dreadfully exaggerated—especially the CRUEL parts.

In these days (when so many are criticizing the behavior of young people, and CRIME) to show a film like this is unbelievable to my way of thinking.

I was born and raised in South Africa, and my father was educated in England, and I find it hard to believe that the youth of that generation were such awful bullies and cowards.

There are so many lovely old books and films that could be shown—WHY SHOW MORE SADISTIC CRIME?

On the evening news you have reports or updates of sewage problems in the city. I don't think it is right to have this on at this time because people are eating and don't want to hear about the sewage problems and how the plant is working.

When the weatherman gives the weather forecast his hands are most prominent, waving continuously.

If he has the need to wave his hands so much, he could at least do something constructive, such as sign language for the hard of hearing.

I am writing this letter in a furious fit of apoplectic anger. Twelve minutes ago, I tuned into Monday Night Baseball in the hopes of perhaps catching a half-way decent National League contest.

Who was I kidding? I was, of course, met by the brassy tones of Keith Jackson, announcing that the featured contest would be between none other than the

Baltimore Orioles and the New York Yankees. May I note that this is the third consecutive week in which the Yankees have been on the main telecast. Heavens, I said to myself, reprovingly, how could I possibly expect anything else? Are not the New York Yankees the most fabulous, fascinating, amazing, stupendous, marvelous, controversial group of professional ath-a-letes God has ever seen fit to place on this earth? Do they not richly deserve to be piped nauseatingly into my living room every Monday evening from April to October? *Of course!*

I am not ticked off at the Yankees per se, even though they possess the shabbiest, most pompously self-serving operation in organized baseball. Rather, I am more steamed at ABC Sports. Do they seriously believe that every single baseball fan in the nation wants desperately to gag on endless Yankee telecasts, with a few interviews with Danny Thomas and the mechanic who once rotated the tires of the car of the nephew of a close friend of the man who managed Elmira for two weeks during the 1969 season?

I know that no amount of protest short of firebombing could reduce the swelling in Roone Garbage's head, but I'm still hoping that you can be convinced to opt for a different game instead of the force-fed Yankee crap particularly since most baseball fans don't give a tinker's damn about the New York Yankees in the first place, just as long as they lose and continue to wallow in the fetid mire of their own egomaniacal outbursts.

I would much prefer a good, stultifying Padres-

Astros game to the swirl of rectum-emptying hyperbole to which the viewer of a Yankee game is subjected.

To whom it may concern: I *demand* you put on FURY!!! If you don't put on Fury then your a dumbell, dirty, stinking RAT!!!

Ask anybody who knows anything about movies and film history, and you'll find they're apt to declare Jean Renoir's "The Rules of the Game" as "the greatest movie ever made."

I was delighted to see "The Rules of the Game" scheduled this evening on public television. And absolutely furious when, as the picture built to its magnificent climax, the last fifteen minutes were lopped off and replaced by a commercial for a program about offshore oil drilling.

I called the local station immediately, and was informed that it was "the traffic department's decision." It was suggested I might call back Tuesday and lodge a formal complaint.

Well, to repeat exactly what I said on the phone: You stupid bastards, you'll never get another dime from me.

I am surprised that you will take off the air good programs and put on SOAP which attacks meaning of life, destruction of high morals of this country, and what is sacred to good-living people.

Why are you so money mad that you don't care for Judeo or Christian morals? Why do you cater to low living standards?

If you must put on low standards of living which is ruining our country, why not put it on at a late hour when most decent living people have retired.

II

Letters to Authors, Editors, and Literary Agents

To the editor of The Drama Review, *New York, upon submission of a manuscript for publication*

Please consider this one-act play for publication. This is a carbon but no one else is considering the play at this time. I have had to type the damn thing over six times already because everyone I send it to keeps it forever and I end up sending queries and more queries and never get the damn thing back and I end up withdrawing it and never never never do I get the damn thing back. So you can type it over yourself, because I refuse to do it again, or you can take it or you can leave it. You people are quick to talk about writers presenting a professional clean copy of a manuscript and then you act like a bunch of inconsiderate fucking assholes yourselves!

To an aspiring dramatist, from Sir Herbert Beerbohm Tree

My Dear Sir, I have read your play.
Oh, my dear Sir.

To a literary agent in New York who had endeavored without success to sell an author's first novel and had thereupon advised him, regretfully, that it was being returned

I have not received the two copies of my novel—those you peddlers refer to as "projects"—nor have I received any insurance data on their shipment.

I doubt that you did insure my works, you have made it quite clear to me they have no more value to you than they have to those charnel houses calling themselves publishing houses from which rises the stench of dead art murdered by the illiterates, the depraved, and other literary street walkers bedizened as editors for whom art is such a threat they kill it with the dagger of their own pretentiousness.

At least this cloying contact with you—however much it has set back my writing, as it has months—has made me realize how hopeless is the status of the artist in this society which is so sick it profits the assassins of its own cultural life blood.

Permit me to thank you for alerting me so pragmatically to that. I can offset that with what you have cost me in writing. But at the same time believe me I hold you responsible for the cost—to me—of my works if they are lost.

To the literary agent, again

It is now too late for my manuscripts to arrive. The post office tells me the odds are practically 100% you never mailed them in the first place, otherwise they would have arrived here in six weeks or be returned there. Your failure to insure them is prima facie evidence of negligence, and indeed, malice, even if you did mail them.

It is too late because I have had to now move towards replacing them, the six weeks loss of their use due to your gross negligence is reason enough. As my third copy is insufficient for photocopying or a typist I am having to take my time from my work to type another original—which many publishers require. This takes weeks.

You will pay for my time and damages and for the loss of creativity your tactics have cost me. You will hear from my people in the East on this matter and if you refuse to pay for the damages you have cost me I shall take you to court. My damages I estimate as $50,000.00.

To anyone reckless enough to send in an unsolicited and unpublishable manuscript to Rolling Stone *magazine, from Hunter Thompson, alias "Raoul Duke, Minister of Manuscripts" for* Rolling Stone

You worthless acid-sucking piece of illiterate *shit*! Don't *ever* send this kind of brain-damaged swill around here again! If I had the time, I'd come out there and drive a fucking wooden stake through your skull! Why don't you get a job, wino? Like maybe punching tickets or delivering the *Shopping News*. You (name of city here) assholes are all the same—just like those cocksuckers at *Rolling Stone*. I could kill those bedwetting geeks for sending me this tedious and embarrassing tissue of delusions . . . and I wouldn't mind killing you, too. Stick this manuscript where it belongs: up your ass.

To the editor of New West *magazine, Los Angeles, when he was slow to return the calls of a literary agent*

This office called you on both Tuesday and Friday of last week and a manuscript was sent round to the

New West office by messenger at the behest of one of your colleagues. To now there has been no reply whatsoever from you.

We do not know who you think you are or just where you think you are but one thing is and should be very clear—in *this* town *my* calls get returned.

As you insist in being an asshole you have our every assurance that you will be treated like one until such time, if ever, that the contrary is established. There is no room on what could not be described as a blooming literary scene for another shitweasel who thinks he is too good for negotiations. We here have had quite enough of that ilk. One more pigfucker is too much.

To Gertrude Stein, from a London publisher to whom she had submitted an unpublished work and who had remained steadfastly unimpressed by her repetitive prose technique ("... a rose is a rose is a rose ...")

I am only one, only one, only one. Only one being, one at the same time. Not two, not three, only one. Only one life to live, only sixty minutes in one hour. Only one pair of eyes. Only one brain. Only one being. Being only one, having only one pair of eyes, having only one time, having only one life, I cannot read your MS. three or four times. Not even one time. Only one look, only one look is enough. Hardly one copy would sell here, hardly one. Hardly one.

Many thanks. I am returning the MS. by registered post. Only one MS. by one post.

To would-be contributors to Hustler *magazine, from the editors of* Hustler, *after determining that the submission in question is unsuitable for publication (the message is printed, in brown, on a drawing of a roll of toilet paper)*

THIS AIN'T
THE KIND
OF SHIT
WE'RE
LOOKING FOR!

To Truth *magazine, from Oscar Wilde, 1890, after the publication of a letter accusing Wilde of plagiarism*

I can hardly imagine that the public are in the very smallest degree interested in the shrill shrieks of "Plagiarism" that proceed from time to time out of the lips of silly vanity or incompetent mediocrity.

However, as Mr. James Whistler has had the impertinence to attack me with both venom and vulgarity in your columns, I hope you will allow me to state that the assertions contained in his letters are as deliberately untrue as they are deliberately offensive.

The definition of a disciple as one who has the courage of the opinions of his master is really too old even for Mr. Whistler to be allowed to claim it, and as for borrowing Mr. Whistler's ideas about art, the only thoroughly original ideas I have ever heard him express have had reference to his own superiority as a painter over painters greater than himself.

It is a trouble for any gentleman to have to notice the lucubrations of so ill-bred and ignorant a person as Mr. Whistler, but your publication of his insolent letter left me no option in the matter.

To Alexander Pope, from Colley Cibber, after Pope had added this memorable quatrain to the torrent of ridicule that continuously poured over the forlorn and untalented poet laureate:

In merry Old England, it once was the Rule,
The King has his Poet, and also his Fool.
But now we're so frugal, I'd have you to know it,
That Cibber can serve both for Fool and for Poet.

If I am the King's Fool, now, Sir, pray, whose fool are you?

To Ralph Waldo Emerson, from Algernon Swinburne, 1874, upon hearing that Emerson had called him "a mere sodomite"

I am informed that certain American journalists, not content with providing filth of their own for the consumption of their kind, sometimes offer to their readers a dish of beastliness which they profess to have gathered from under the chairs of more distinguished men.

I am not sufficiently expert in the dialect of the cesspool and the dung-cart to retort in their own kind on these venerable gentlemen—I, whose ears and lips alike are unused to the amenities of conversation embroidered with such fragments of flowery rhetoric as may be fished up by congenial fingers or lapped up by congenial tongues out of the sewage of Sodom . . .

A foul mouth is so ill-matched with a white beard that I would gladly believe the newspaper scribes alone responsible for the bestial utterances which they declare to be dropped from a teacher whom such disciples as these exhibit to our disgust and compassion as performing on their obscene platform the last tricks of tongue now possible to a gap-toothed and hoary-headed ape, carried at first into notice on the shoulder of Carlyle, and who now in his dotage spits and chatters from a dirtier perch of his own finding and fouling: coryphaeus or choragus of his Bulgarian tribe of autocoprophagous baboons, who make the filth they feed on.

To Jon Carroll, West Coast columnist and editor, from a young lady, after Mr. Carroll had written an article in the San Francisco Examiner *suggesting, in what soon proved to be an understatement, that Elvis Presley was past his prime*

To me your just a jealous old man who probably is ugly who would appreciate women screaming Jon Jon Jon we love you Jon. Well baby let me tell you you will get no where bad wrapping people.

And further more you have the power of the press backing you up a hundred percent so keep talking bad about people and you'll find nobody screaming Jon Jon we love you and remember there are other younger reporters who might not like you who will talk bad about you and remember your tombstone might read

Jon Carroll the bad wrapper

To Richard Meltzer, journalist and rock music critic, following the publication of an article in which he expressed some misgivings about Paul McCartney's musicality and, indeed, masculinity

The other day, I was at a newsstand with a friend, when suddenly she cried out, "Jesus, there is some jerk named Meltzer around, cutting down Paul McCartney!!!"

Listen, bud, we've never heard of you . . . or your kind. We've heard of critics, but this is hitting below the belt. Who died and made you king??? That you would have the audacity to slam Paul McCartney. Years from now, hundreds of years, people will be studying him and his music, and he will be looked back upon as one of the world's geniuses, and you can't even be remembered ten measly years from now. You no talent slob.

What was wrong with being singled out as a sex symbol? He was one then, and is one now. And you have the gall to call him a faggot!!! It's plain as day, you birdbrain. It is our guess that you are a homosexual, and once upon a time, dreamed of having Paul as your lover. When he didn't give you a tumble, you became viciously enraged, and have devoted your whole stupid life to making Paul look bad. It's a waste of time, creep. A no-count, two-bit snake like you never made a king look bad.

You're not fit for Paul to spit on!!! You aren't fit for him to use as toilet paper. You are lower than a pregnant snake's belly!!! Why don't you quit while it's still up to you . . . before the Beatlemaniacs of the universe descend upon you with hatchets, whips, and chains. And believe me, there are enough Beatlefreaks to take care of you forever.

You have a ½-horsepower brain, pulling a two-ton mouth, and you had better watch what comes out, before the Beatle fans of the world rebel.

To Richard Meltzer, after he had confessed in a column to an unfortunate lapse of urinary control during a concert

So you're the bastard who pissed in his seat at the Ritz Theatre! You're the same kind of guy who makes it a practice to fuck in a cesspool.

You never could write a review worth shit.

To the editor of Creem *magazine, from a gentleman who considered that he had been grossly maligned in that magazine*

I am writing this letter, providing procedure whereby my name was reviewed in your magazine in the January issue.

I am the said imposter who took the name of Mr. David Bowie, the British rock star & actor. I impose your magazine with regard of not a true fact or facts, about my statutory classification which arbitrarily excludes some but not all of those similarly situated in relation to legitimate purpose of my stature does not necessarily invalidate entire true facts, about my matter, or my look-alike, this confused me and I know it confused the real "David Bowie"!

I request your magazine better look into this matter, this is very important, and get this *mess* of such defendant under a commitment issued here—under my name, upon which defendant was delivered to prison for one count of 3056 P.C. in violation of one count of parole—not 18 counts of parole violation. I am in prison for a six month term, one count of parole by the act of failing to keep my agent informed as to my whereabouts.

Sir, I am "highly irritated" by this magazine. I didn't score $250,000 in cash and securities, also didn't scam a trip to Hawaii, this is verifiable by my parole officer and Los Angeles Police Dept. I have never impersonated Mr. Bowie, my friends just think I am the freaky British rock star because of my look-alike!

To music critic Paul Hume, from President Harry S. Truman, after Mr. Hume had characterized the singing of the President's daughter, Margaret Truman, in unflattering terms

I have just read your lousy review in the back pages. You sound like a frustrated old man who never made a success, an eight-ulcer man on a four-ulcer job, and all four ulcers working. I have never met you, but if I do you'll need a new nose and plenty of beefsteak and perhaps a supporter below. Westbrook Pegler, a guttersnipe, is a gentleman compared to you. You can take that as more of an insult than as a reflection on your ancestry.

To Erma Bombeck, from readers of Mrs. Bombeck's newspaper column

You gripe about everything. Aspirin bottles that only a two-year-old can open, grocery carts with wheels that go in four different directions, carrying on when the plants in your doctor's office are dead and your stupid ironing board that hasn't been down in ten years. You hate dogs, children and urologists who offer you a drink. You're sick!

P.S. I never read you!

I was married to a shrew like you once for three days.

(EDITOR'S NOTE: Mrs. Bombeck replied to this terse note with the question, "How did you last so long?" The gentleman's even terser response: "I drank.")

To Craig Claiborne, food critic of the New York Times, *after he had described for his readers in gastronomic detail a not inexpensive repast he had enjoyed in Paris*

I was revolted and horrified by your recent article on $4,000.00 spent for a single meal for two. You come off as something of an unfeeling hog. Never was an article more obscene, gross and truly pornographic. In times like these articles like that one hardly are intelligent and win no friends for New York City, for whom the New York Times is chief spokesperson. It will always be possible to be taken for a buggy ride but does the taking have to be described so fully.

Now I know exactly to whom St. Paul was referring when he spoke of those "whose god is their belly." You and your copain, of course. After the $4,000 dinner, you have the gall to write dully and at length about all the courses, all the wines. It serves you right if one of the soups really had shreds of crepes in it.

Regarding the $4000 front page dinner extravaganza —"Let 'em eat cake"—eh, Craig, baby?

Your reply to the people who expressed disgust about your $4000.00 gourmet dinner for two reveals further your complete lack of character and sensitivity.

That you should "feel enormously privileged" about this decadent gorging of food establishes you at the top of moral decay insulting to your newspaper readers. Your analogy to winning a Mercedes-Benz is stupid and illogical. That car would at least serve some practical purpose.

I was delighted to learn this morning that The Times had received "more than 250 letters" as of yesterday regarding your $4,000 dinner feature and that "virtually all were condemnatory."

Mine was one which did not get into print which is really of no concern to me. My revulsion to your article was well expressed by those whose letters did appear.

And the only descriptive word that was included in my letter which wasn't included in the letters I read this morning you, yourself, used in your apology: "obscene." It was an extremely obscene performance—both your consumption of the dinner and your report of it.

I'm certain you read the letters and, perhaps, The Times has sent you those it didn't have space to use.

If you have any sense of responsibility as a human being—which I seriously doubt—you might consider posting the following somewhere you can be reminded of what so many others, like me, feel about you:

absurd
wasteful luxury
extreme frivolity
dissoluteness
decadence
moral decay
debasement
wanton decadence
unconscionable
poor taste
an insult

vulgarity
disgusting
frivolous
evanescent
unredeeming
vulgar
decadent
grossly outraged
indignation
incredible

To V.C. Gilman, a literary critic, from Jack London, after Gilman had been scornful of the author's use of language

My kind kicks authority out of the path. Your kind puts mine in jail for violent assault on authority. My kind makes the living language. Your kind preserves the language my kind makes. Your kind and mine are always at war. We have been so in the past, and we shall be so in the future as long as languages *live* upon the planet. This is not sophistry; it is clubbing home the science of language, and is deeper than the deepest generalisations of the purist and the vulgarist. Think it over.

To William F. Buckley, Jr., from a reader of Mr. Buckley's National Review

Three cheers to Dr. Ross Terrill. He slashed you to bits as you have been doing to yourself for the past year. Cancel my subscription.

(EDITOR'S NOTE: Mr. Buckley replied, "Cancel your own goddamn subscription.")

To the editor of New York *magazine, following publication of an article by Jessica Mitford in which she recounted an extraordinary experience at a well-known Manhattan restaurant*

I happened to be at the restaurant the evening Miss Mitford recalls in her article. Unfortunately she did not mention what a scene she made, and was *drunk.* I feel the manager handled the situation well, considering Miss Mitford was looking to make trouble.

In reply to this week's outrageously uncorrect article by Jessica Mitford, I would like to tell it as I saw it from the table next door.

I feel obliged to say that Miss Mitford was inebriated upon being seated, which she neglected to add in her condemnation of the restaurant.

Miss Mitford is no more qualified to write about funerals than critiquing restaurants.

(EDITOR'S NOTE: A very puzzled and very sober Miss Mitford, after making the chance discovery that both of the above communications were postmarked by the same postage meter, was eventually able to establish that these two letters constituted the only interesting creative writing ever produced by a young lady in the employ of the firm that handled the restaurant's public relations.)

To Philip J. Klass, author of UFOs Explained, *who has generously offered a reward of $10,000 to anyone capable of presenting verifiable proof that extraterrestrial craft have ever landed on this planet*

I saw you on the "Today" show and heard of your offer. I would like to know if you would extend the offer to pay me $10,000 for concrete evidence that space craft "saucers" from other planets do exist and if so what you would accept as concrete evidence.

Not to be unfair, I wish to point out that I live within two miles of a known space craft landing area and have seen them personally and one of my friends has talked (sign) to one of the space men—or women—and walked with him a distance of 600 feet. He has also made a model of the craft.

I would respectfully suggest you dig a hole and keep it handy to jump into when the facts come out.

I have read about your constant skepticism on U.F.O. —"flying saucers."

I resent your attitude very much. You are, no doubt, a nice guy? Which would have no bearing on my opinion of you or your attitude towards all and any U.F.O. encounters and sightings.

It seems to me you live in fatal fear of the truth of U.F.O phenomena. Let me just briefly close this letter by saying to you, sir, that if you would have been with me that night in New Mexico, almost 26 years ago, when the U.F.O crippled my knee, you would have had the living *hell* scared out of you!

To Professor Fredrica Bartz, following publication of an article in which she proposed that teachers, to accommodate the sensibilities of parents who had expressed shock upon discovering sundry vulgar colloquialisms in their children's assigned reading matter, might consider excising from books the pages on which such words occur and pasting them on the walls of the school bathrooms, where the pupils could then repair to expand this area of their vocabularies in a more familiar context

Your article "An Immodest Proposal" published in the latest Teachers' Edition of "Read" has fallen into a *concerned* mothers hands. My hands. It was brought home from school by my ten year old son.

After showing the article to several *concerned* mothers —(nice too) some are teachers—we can only conclude that the article is subversive and we are turning it in to the Federal Bureau of Investigation.

None of us object to Sex Education in schools nor do we object to long hair. We have found obsene literature in our school library which we are relative sure was placed there by an alleged Communist. This woman does not work in the library anymore.

We have found your article shocking, disgusting, and obviously subversive.

P.S. Have you been in the bathroom of every elementary school? I haven't. My son says he has seen only one dirty word on such walls.

To the editor of The Observer, *London, after publication of an article by George Melly*

Perhaps, sir, you would be able to explain to a boy of ten what a wank barrier is. This was the problem I had to face on Sunday afternoon when the boy's mother had said quite honestly that she did not know.

There was no reason why the boy should not have asked the question—after all he has not been brought up amongst people who use such language.

I had not read the article until I was asked the question. I do not see why we have to read such rubbish in what used to be considered an intelligent, decent Sunday newspaper. It will not come into my house again.

To Charles Berlitz, author of The Bermuda Triangle

Mr. Berlitz, You didn't scare *us* with your Bermuda Triangle.

To Elkan Allan, television critic and compiler of the "Critical Viewer's Guide to the Week's Television" in the London Sunday Times

I used to puzzle over your quirkily neurotic outbursts when referring to people like Michael Parkinson and Melvyn Bragg, both of whom can so demonstrably write you into the ground without turning a hair. Then I saw you on a television discussion programme, and realized the awful truth—you desperately want to be a "TV PERSONALITY" yourself.

"Bumptious" is described by Webster's Dictionary as "presumptuously self-assertive," a phrase which, as your weekly column clearly demonstrates, fits you like a glove. To it, I would add "smug," "arrogant," "odious," and "puerile."

I have beside me, as I write, two tubes of glutinous liquid, which, I am told, when mixed, will form an adhesive powerful enough to weld together two elephants who would rather part company and hold up the Clifton Suspension Bridge should it ever run out of suspenders.

I would prefer, however, to put this admirable concoction to a different use. I would like, in fact, to spoon out darn great dollops of it into your beard. "Why?" I hear you asking plaintively as you bend over your typewriter tapping out blurbs for next week's boxwatching. "Why me?"

I shall tell you why I would like to daub your beard with glue and decorate it with all the bits of fluff I have removed from my old Hoover. It is because although you are able to encapsulate genius at work, thus bringing Paradise to millions of viewers who can now see it on BBC 1 ("manic hotel proprietor John Cleese in *Fawlty Towers*"), you are also able to condemn *The Sweeney* on the same page as Thames' London version of *The Streets of San Francisco.*

This, in my view, and I'll lay ten to one it is shared by thousands of *Sunday Times* readers, is like calling Sid the Sardine the Mediterranean version of Moby Dick. The other way about, on second thought.

Have you not yourself fought off death by boredom as Karl Malden, for the millionth time, has said: "Hold it right there, Buster?" (They never do hold it right there. Never. Nor do they *freeze.*) Have you never stifled a scream as old Karl has told "Buddy Boy" (BUDDY BOY? FOR CRIPES SAKE!) for the *millionth time* to get out an A.P.B. on someone and check his M.O.?

Have you been wearing earplugs when *The Sweeney*

comes on? (Lee Montague, just out of the nick, to his ten-year-old daughter: "What do you want to be when you grow up?" Little girl: "A social worker.")

I shall go to church today and ask God to give me patience enough to pick up the Critical Viewers' Guide and read it without screaming. I hope you will do your best, therefore, to ensure that I shall not need to bite the carpet before I am force-fed six tranquilisers for lunch by my wife. Otherwise there is nothing for it but a visit to the *Sunday Times* office, armed with my Neverslack adhesive. They say you can dab it on the wheels of Concorde and ground it for life. Think what it does for beards. Come, Mr. Allan; there must be hope for someone like yourself who thinks that the Muppets are "super characters." We would probably agree (we had better, if my Neverslack is not to be brought into action) that Dougall, of *Magic Roundabout* fame, is a better philosopher than Malcolm Muggeridge. Just retract that bit about *The Sweeney* and all will be forgiven.

To Anthony Haden-Guest, New York journalist and bon vivant

Now I know why you have such a foul reputation among other writers in this city. Your latest "piece" in the new *Chic* magazine is a direct rip-off of the article Rose Mary Kent did in *New York* magazine last spring. You are the king of rip-off and not even an imaginative, honest one. If you were a gentleman, as you are always trying to promote yourself, you would have suggested Miss Kent do the article herself since it was her idea to begin with, not yours.

To the editor of New York *magazine, after publication of an article by Anthony Haden-Guest on the financier Bernard Cornfeld*

Anthony Haden-Guest's article on Bernie Cornfeld was the most fawning, sycophantic load of bullshit I have read for a long time. What does he do? Owe Bernie money or something? On second thoughts, Bernie probably procures girls for him. Apart from the article, WHO ON EARTH was that hideously ugly guy in the mirror behind Bernie? That's like finding a piece of SHIT in a Coquille St. Jacques.

(EDITOR'S NOTE: The "guy in the mirror" was Mr. Haden-Guest.)

To John Simon, drama critic of New York *magazine, after he had passed unfavorable comment on the facial appearance and acting ability of Liza Minnelli*

You have obviously spent so much time with your head wedged between your buttocks that your vision has been obscured by the reflection of your own putrid entrails.

If the art of literary or dramatic criticism is to remain viable, we must seek to eliminate people like you who degrade the art form by taking cheap shots at performers' physical liabilities and who must darkly illuminate their critiques with pseudo-intellectual name calling.

If you must persist in deriding Ms. Minnelli's so called imperfections, at least do so with the stroke of your pen rather than with the excrement of your bowels.

You have no more right to say an uncivil thing than to act one. In ridiculing Liza's looks, you clearly exhibited your heartless malignity. How can one be held responsible for the structure of one's face? You aren't satisfied criticizing performers, now you're criticizing God.

I always thought your brain deserving—of first prize in the spaghetti category. You're a pathetic—probably paranoid—individual whose vituperative reviews become less credible with each pointless attack on a performer's nose, chin, hairline . . . whatever!

You need help. They should get you to the Old Critic's Home. Quick! And they should take away all sharp instruments, like your typewriter.

Of course, I haven't figured out, just yet, what can be done about your tongue.

I have never had the pleasure of meeting Miss Minnelli personally, however, I have had the privilege of seeing her in performance twice, most recently in "The Act."

I was always impressed with the fact that Miss Minnelli was such a lady, always dignified and never succumbing to the applause-winning exploitation that she could so easily make a living off of. The fact that she is exceptionally talented goes without saying.

I have never considered myself a gentleman. So, on behalf of Miss Minnelli, in response to your incredibly unprofessional piece of yellow journalism, I wish to express the following sentiment:

FUCK YOU, FAGGOT

I suppose when you review "Cheaters," you will accuse Lou Jacobi and Jack Weston of being fat and funny looking.

To Nelson Doubleday, from Alexander Woollcott, after Mr. Doubleday's publishing firm had advertised a novel by Kenneth Roberts about the American Revolution as being a work of history

There has been sticking in my crop for several days the notion that I, presumably one of many, should send you a word of protest about an advertisement of *Oliver Wiswell* which I saw in the *Times*, on the daily book-page, a week or so ago. I refer to the one in which that curious piece of fiction was blandly presented by your publishing house as the long suppressed historical truth which had been "banned" from our text books. Of course you and I know that this is—if I may reach for the *mot juste*—horseshit.

Kenneth's new and retroactive Toryism is an interesting psychiatric case. His own state of mind enabled him to write, with passionate conviction, a good story of the American Revolution from the Tory point of view. It is about as faithful a *history* of the Revolution as would be an account of the last eight years in the White House written by Alice Longworth. You were right and lucky to publish *Oliver Wiswell* but for your firm to adopt and endorse the viewpoint of its protagonist in your effort to sell copies of the book strikes me as nothing short of degrading and shameful.

Trusting that you have long since crapped all over the dimwit responsible, I beg to remain . . .

To Eleanor Roosevelt, from Alexander Woollcott, after the President's wife had written that she had been depressed by Thornton Wilder's play Our Town

And now, as your senior and better in dramatic criticism, let me make a word of comment on your progress as a playgoer. The late Charles Frohman used to say that sometimes it wasn't the play that failed, but the public. I gather from your diary that when you went to see *Our Town* you were not at your best. I am afraid you didn't give what I could conscientiously call a good performance. If at that gentle masterpiece, you were "depressed beyond words," it must have been on some evening when you would not have been spiritually equal to reading, let us say, Gray's *Elegy*.

So now this is what you must do. You must eat some lettuce, read a little Charles Lamb, take a nap and go to see *Our Town* again. After that, kindly report to me at once and oblige.

To Lord Willis, English author

Sir, I have just finished reading your strange mixture of fact and fiction, *Whatever Happened to Tom Mix*?

The answer of course is that he died, a very strange ending for a human being, don't you think?

Quite an interesting book of its kind, but there is no need to expose your bollocks when writing about your early sexual experiences, because nobody is in the least interested, and it does not help to sell the book, which

I suppose is the only reason you wrote it, i.e. to make a little money.

To the editor of Los Angeles *magazine*

Gentlemen—please take us off the list for the complimentary copy of your fucking magazine.

Thank you.

To a columnist for the journal Ami des Lois, *from the Marquis de Sade, 1799, following the publication of a premature obituary in which the "late" Marquis was condemned as the author of the scandalous novel* Justine

No, I am not dead, and I would like to imprint proof of my unequivocal existence on your shoulders with a very vigorous stick. I would do so, in fact, did I not fear the plague miasma of your mephitic corpse. But when all is said and done, scorn is the only weapon that a decent man need use to repel the banalities of a blockhead like yourself.

It is not true that I am the author of *Justine*. To any

other than a dolt such as you I might take the trouble to prove this, but what emerges from your stinking mouth is so stupid that refutation would dishonor more than accusation.

A sensible man, when barked at by curs of your type, spits on them and continues on his way.

So bark away, bray, howl, brew your poison; your inability, like that of the toad, to spit beyond your own nose, causing it to fall back on yourself, will succeed in covering but yourself with the poison you would like to sully others with.

III

Letters to Corporations and Businesses

To the Hartford Electric Light Company, from Mark Twain

There are but two places in our whole street where lights could be of any value, by any accident, and you have measured and appointed your intervals so ingeniously as to leave each of those places in the centre of a couple of hundred yards of solid darkness. When I noticed that you were setting one of your lights in such a way that I could almost see how to get into my gate at night, I suspected that it was a piece of carelessness on the part of the workmen, and would be corrected as soon as you should go around inspecting and find it out. My judgment was right; it is always right, when you are concerned. For fifteen years, in spite of my prayers and tears, you persistently kept a gas lamp exactly half way between my gates, so that I couldn't find either of them after dark; and then furnished such execrable gas that I had to hang a danger signal on the lamp post to keep teams from running into it, nights.

Now I suppose your present idea is to leave us a little more in the dark.

Don't mind us—out our way, we possess but one vote apiece, and no rights which you are in any way bound to respect. Please take your electric light and go to—but never mind, it is not for me to suggest; you will probably find the way; and any way you can reasonably count on divine assistance if you lose your bearings.

Some day you will move me almost to the verge of irritation by your chuckle-headed Goddamned fashion of shutting your Goddamned gas off without giving any notice to your Goddamned parishioners. Several times you have come within an ace of smothering half of this household in their beds and blowing up the other half by this idiotic, not to say criminal, custom of yours. And it has happened again to-day. Haven't you a telephone?

To Consolidated Edison, the New York power company, after the blackout of July, 1977

I just want to take the time to thank you for your two latest customer service ideas. I think the idea of using the intimacy and coziness of candlelight to bring New Yorkers together in our city's troubled times is a great one. And I also love your "instant home defrost service," wherein everyone in the city can defrost their freezers at the same time. I might also add that in this era of critical energy shortages, your new services are a great way to conserve vital energy supplies.

To Consolidated Edison

This morning I had been home from work and became aware of the asininity of one of your meter readers.

The front doorbell rang and I went to the door to answer it. There was no one. Five minutes later the doorbell rang again. I went to the door. There was no one. I went to the steps to look down at other houses. Three houses down there was this man ringing doorbells never stopping but moving along.

I called out to him and asked if he rang the bell. He replied, "Con Edison. Meter reader." I shouted back and asked why he didn't wait for the owner to get the answer. His answer, "Man, *I gotta keep moving*!"

Is Con Edison now in the role of playing Halloween games? Are you playing "ring the bell and run"? I played that as a kid. I've grown up and I certainly hope Con Ed has too!

Finally, my meter can be read from the outside. Outside my garage door there is an extension of my meter which the reader can gain his reading. There's no need to make my wife or me part of the game of "ring the bell and run." I'm too busy using Con Ed energy reading good books.

To a department store in Pittsburgh

I am writing to you of the Raw & Rank deal I got from your local store. Every time I went in or my daughter went in my behalf they kept stalling me. I happened to be in the said mentioned store with my daughter and heard and seen what goes on. When a customer purchases merchandise and it's in the store, someone else comes in, and is known to your rotten help, and requests the same merchandise as the previous customer, me, the second customer gets it, and the clerk in the store says they'll reorder for the customer that originally requested same, me.

You should get more reliable help. I'm finished with your firm.

To a manufacturer of canned soup

I must share with you my experience with your chicken soup. It may give you some new marketing ideas. Let me explain . . .

Recently I had a cold and everyone suggested things like aspirin, hot tea with honey, and CHICKEN SOUP!

Now, all my appropriate soup making pots were in the refrigerator filled with other things and I realized that I had nothing in which to prepare the soup. I looked around and the only available pot was a glass coffee pot that I occasionally use to boil water. The reason that I "occasionally" use this pot is that it had these ugly brown stains that I couldn't manage to clean off.

In fact, two days before I decided to attack this ugly brown grunge with (in order of use) 1. dish detergent 2. Comet Cleanser 3. Brillo. I scrubbed and scrubbed but those stains wouldn't budge.

Wanting to prepare the soup, I figured that the stains in the pot wouldn't do my body much damage since they weren't about to come off—ever.

Well, I followed the package directions and let it become soup for the designated length of time. I smelled it brewing. I then ladeled out a cup full and as I sniffed and blew my nose my eyes opened wide and I stopped!

My coffee pot looked different. It was clear. I actually saw the broth and noodles swimming around. WHERE WAS THE BROWN STAIN?

Intrigued, I poured out the rest of the soup into a container so that I could have a better look.

There was my brown grungy coffee pot—SPARKLING CLEAN!

Nothing that Proctor and Gamble or Palmolive makes or plain old elbow grease could do the same cleaning job of your Chicken Soup!

I'd like to ask a few questions: 1. Just what is the secret ingredient that goes into the soup that could do such a fantastic job on grime? 2. What is that product doing to my body? 3. Am I supposed to drink this when I feel like soup or every 3,000 miles?

To an electronic equipment store in Detroit

After having to keep coming back several times to exchange tape recorders the recorder I have now is Sound Wave model no. P-846F. You did not give me a guarantee. When I brought it back to the store I told the salesman with the black goatee that I need a guarantee, and he said "quit trying to hand me your bullshit." After he pulled a guarantee out of a box and gave it to me I left. When I got home I discovered that the model no. on it was for something else. The recorder I have is breaking very bad. I want a new machine for being cursed at.

To the head office of a fast-food restaurant chain

At about 6:00 p.m., Saturday, July 20th, my wife, daughter and I had occasion to patronize one of your restaurants.

We all ordered Spaghetti & Meatball Dinners, but were informed there was no more Spaghetti. I then ordered a Ground Beef Dinner, my daughter ordered a Chicken Dinner while my wife studied the menu. The waitress returned saying they were out of Chicken. My daughter then ordered the Ground Beef Dinner and my wife ordered Knockwurst with Potato Pancakes. Once again the waitress returned saying they didn't have any Potato Pancakes. My wife then ordered the Deluxe Sandwich. My daughter and I are now eating our meal as the waitress returned saying they are out of Turkey. Needless to say, by now, my wife is furious and would not attempt to order anything else.

The three of us should have departed at that point, but my daughter and I finished our meal.

After our meal, my wife and daughter went to the Ladies Room while I paid the bill. They returned saying, the toilet is over-flowing and there is water all over the floor.

If this is any way to run a restaurant, I fail to see it.

To the New York Telephone Company

First you steal my September payment and lose it in the mail and now Mr. Nick of your repair service is accusing me of making up trouble on my line to avoid paying the bill. Today my outgoing calls were cut off.

If the accusation isn't retracted and an answer isn't given me I will sue you for the damage afflicted on me.

To the head office of a supermarket chain

I would like to make a complaint about your Big Rip-Off and about New York City restaurants in general.

I very seldom eat out in *any* restaurant for two reasons: First, I can't afford them and second they generally overcharge you especially when you have a date and know it's too embarrassing to complain and spoil making an impression on your date.

In the past several months I have collected a number of your coupons that entitle me to a free dinner each time I purchase $10.00 worth of groceries.

I took a date to a restaurant on June 18th. The cheapest meal was a chop steak for $9.00. All I got was the chop steak and french fried potatoes. My date ordered Lobster for $12.00. We had two salads, two cups of coffee and no desert. The bill was $25.00. I was given credit for $10.50.

On July 17th, I took a date to another restaurant. My date ordered a steak with a salad and order of spinach. I ordered scallops with french fries and a salad. I had cheese cake and coffee for desert. My date had only another salad for desert. Her steak was listed at $11.00 and my scallops were listed at $9.00. The total bill was $32.00. I paid $16.50 plus a three dollar tip.

I could have gone to a number of restaurants without this "big deal" coupon and paid less and got a better meal.

This is nothing but a racket and con job to rip off the public. Also, I haven't heard of anyone winning any money in your Big Money Game.

To a dating service in Atlanta, from a disappointed spinster in her middle years

A month ago I paid you $35.00 and you haven't given me one date so far. I don't believe you even have anyone for me, because every time I call to see what you are doing for me I am told to call back later as you have no one to give my name to.

I feel as though I have been taken for a ride. If you had no one for me you should have told me so, not just take my money.

To a manufacturer of firearms, from a gentleman who had previously written to make known his unhappiness at not having received a gun he had ordered 36 months before

I have just received a reply from your Product Manager and quite frankly it serves no purpose, offers no solution, gives no concrete commitment, and placates me none at all. Basically it says nothing but keep on waiting you poor slob, which only adds to my dissatisfaction. Two and one half years is not very long to wait, if I read the second paragraph correctly.

The letter says that deliveries are made in chronological order. Are you, if this is true, two and one half years behind in your deliveries? I think not, or your stockholders would certainly be bailing out from under a company that cannot produce an ordered item within two and one half years.

The letter also says that law enforcement orders are given priority of delivery. This means to me that for two and one half years all your orders have been going to police officers. If that is true each one must be packing around a lot of hardware. I hope I'm on their side when the shooting starts as I'm the only one without something to shoot with.

To a hardware store in Denver

This is about a toilet seat I purchased at your store. The item number is 103 and the price $5.59. It lasted two months and this is mighty expensive to last for such a short time. The screws were very short so that the top part couldn't be kept on. It falls off all the time. You better take it back.

To the American Kennel Club

I received your letter, and I think you people don't know what you are doing. Because on the papers you sent me did not mention anything about having to have there parents AKC number. Now are you guys up there going to sit back and tell me a bunch of bull? Well if that's the way you people run your business that is really bad.

I am being to think that you people don't like dogs or people who are will to pay the fee to have her *PURE BREED COCKER SPANIEL*! registered.

I told you about my friend who has a dog. Well she didn't have the AKC number of the dogs parents. And you people didn't give her any bull that you are giving me. So you can do what ever you want to do, but I will get my dog registered.

Do you know that there is a place for people like you and who ever the another people are that's giving me a hard time. And you people are giving me a bad time, because I can tell when someone is giving me a bad time. I hope you are all having fun doing this.

You people must be really hard up to be giving me a bad time. I hope you think about what I said. Why can't you just give me a number of my own for my *PURE BREED COCKER SPANIEL*! I don't think it would kill you to give me a number of my own. I will go to the person at the top if I have to get some business out of you people at the American Kennel Club.

If you still don't think my dog is a Pure Breed send

a person out here to California and look at my dog, if you want to spend some money, but if I know you people it would cost too much money to send a person.

Tell me something, when a person has a Pure Breed dog that is not registered with the AKC but wants to register what does the person do? I am trying to be nice about what I am writing but it is hard when a person is mad because someplace or someone is giving me a hard time.

I can't tell you everything I want to because you could get me trouble.

If my dog wasn't a *PURE BREED COCKER SPANIEL* I would not be trying to get her registered. But she is a Pure Breed Cocker! So I am trying to get her registered. I will pay you the $5.00 if you let me register my dog.

If you still don't think my dog is a Pure Breed Cocker Spaniel like I said before you can send someone to look over my dog.

To George Whitman, the proprietor of Shakespeare & Co., a celebrated bookshop in Paris once frequented by Hemingway, Joyce, Henry Miller, Gertrude Stein, and other literary notables

My publisher and I visited your establishment several weeks ago and found you such a preposterous boor that

I was moved to discourse upon the likes of you in the attached interview with the *Washington Star*. The next time I am in Paris, I intend to spread cream cheese all over your collection.

To a travel agency in Milwaukee

I recently returned from a vacation in Europe where my husband and I arranged hotel accommodation through you in Innsbruck, Austria; Vienna, Austria; Munich, Germany; Amsterdam, Holland; and Brussels, Belgium.

When I arrived in Innsbruck, I was shocked at the hotel. The toilets were disgusting and an intense odor of urine permeated the entire bathroom. It was impossible to use the toilet facilities. The windows of our room had double glass and in one window, the outer glass was missing. The weather was very cold and bitter and the freezing cold air filled our room. Luckily, this cold air circulated the urine smelling air that came from the bathroom since our room was next to the bathroom.

In addition, many Swedish children ran up and down the halls in their clogs as they slammed doors at nighttime.

I asked the children to be quiet as a good night's sleep is a prerequisite before a full day of sightseeing. They did not care and continued to make noise.

The greatest shock awaited us when we entered the hotel in Vienna. You described the hotel as an excellent, clean, small hotel. The minute we walked in the front door, a rancid odor greeted us. These bathrooms stunk of urine and at night there was no light in the bathroom. For the three days we stayed at the hotel, the light was never replaced. The bathtub was filthy and had bugs in it. When my husband took a nap in the lumpy bed, he awoke to find a bug on his arm. The dishes at breakfast were filthy. I innocently put a lemon in my tea. When I picked the lemon out of the dish, the bottom of the dish was covered with black specks. In the room, the hot water usually went off and it was impossible to wash our face or our clothes. In the room, the electrical wires of the chandelier were exposed which must be a fire hazard. The walls of the room were paper thin and sounds of your neighbor reverberated everywhere. When the trolley passed in the street, the room shook.

Even though our hotel in Brussels had flies in the room, plaster peeling off the walls and exposed electrical wire, the bathrooms did not smell and were usable. The dishes at breakfast were also clean. Therefore, the hotel was adequate.

However, our stays in Innsbruck and Vienna were ruined because of the discomfort experienced from your accommodations. How can you compensate us for ruining these two cities on our first European trip? It is difficult to find a materialistic figure that would compensate for this. All I can request is to be reimbursed for the hotels that you negligently recommended and endorsed as providing clean rooms and bathrooms. In addition, several other expenses were incurred due to your negligence. Listed below is an itemized list of expenses that I expect to be reimbursed for:

Innsbruck

Hotel Fee	$34.00 for one night
One night's sleep - cold incurred due to window	Priceless
Medicine due to cold	3.00
Aggravation	Priceless

Vienna

Hotel Fee	$60.00
Pay toilets used	1.50
Stomach pains	Priceless
Diarrhea medicine	1.00
Tablets for indigestion	.65
Bad breath mints (due to stomach problems)	.30
Aggravation in Vienna	Priceless
Interruption of sightseeing	Priceless

How can you compensate for ruining a stay in a European city? Could you mail us plane tickets for Vienna and Innsbruck and enclose decent hotel accomodations? That is the fair thing to do!

At least I expect to receive $100.45 total reimbursement for negligent services AND AN ADDITIONAL AMOUNT DETERMINED BY YOU FOR EMOTIONAL DAMAGES.

To a dress manufacturer in New York

On July 27th, 1964, I purchased two dresses at an apparel store handling your merchandise in Omaha. At the end of the purchase the saleswoman said "these dresses are not returnable."

After I got home I began to hang up the dresses and noticed the white dress had black spots in the back of it. I returned the dress to the store right away and the saleswoman said it was nothing, and that she would have the spots taken care of, and to pick the dress up the next day. I returned to the store to pick the dress up and still the spots did not come off. She suggested she would take a few dollars off and have the dress cleaned. I told her I wouldn't take the chance and what if the spots didn't come off after having it cleaned, especially since she tried to clean them off. By the way, these dresses were *not* purchased at a sale price.

Now getting to the other dress, this print dress. I took this dress to Baltimore for my sister's *shower*, which was on the August 2nd weekend. I put this dress on at 6:30, arrived at the shower at 7:15. At around 8 o'clock that evening my mother came up to me and said my dress was torn. I looked about me and could not see anything that could have snagged to tear it. I was quite upset as it was the only dressy dress I brought with me and I wanted to wear it for another occasion. When I got home I tried to mend it so that I could wear it. In trying to mend it, it ravelled. By then I was exasperated so when I returned to Omaha that week I took it to the store and explained to the saleswoman what happened and told her I couldn't understand how it happened, but through handling and me trying to fix it it ravelled more.

I asked the saleswoman if she could get more material and that I would repanel it. The saleswoman said there was no more of same material. She suggested taking it to dressmaker and the dressmaker said there was nothing she could do. I returned to the store and told the saleswoman this dress is useless and then the owner came and said that I definitely snagged the dress, by then I was ready to burst, so I told her that my husband refuses to pay for a dress that was only worn for a couple of hours. If it were a cigarette burn, or a definite snag, he could see that it was the fault of a nail or whatever caused the snag. But to wear a dress to a shower with many other women present and no one else snagging their dress on the same seats I sat on is unexplainable. If it was the seat I would have had more snags in that area, as I had gotten up and sat down in the same seat several times. The other saleswomen in the store said to take it to my insurance company, so I told her I was returning this dress to the manufacturer and let them make it useful, as I've never had this happen to me before, especially since I didn't wear it to go on a hike or a picnic.

That's why there's a dress with this letter.

To an electronic equipment store in Chicago

Today I went to your store and I would like whomever is responsible to be aware of the inconsiderate service I received there.

I went to buy a bottle of "head cleaner" for my tape recorder. In asking for it the person serving quickly obtained what I sought and then suggested the kit which includes the "cue tips." I replied that I already bought the kit so I have the cue tips and only need the head cleaner. Besides, I said, the kit is more expensive. The salesman frowned impolitely.

He then proceeded to write up a receipt. The salesman asked for my name. I replied, "No, you cannot have it."

He then frowned again (which, of course, is certainly not courteous), took my money, placed the bottle and receipt on the counter and walked away. He and one of the younger workers were not busy helping other customers, so I feel the following actions he made are inexcusable.

I then requested a bag. He replied, "No." I waited to see if any of the salespeople would help—and I asked again, "May I please have a paper bag for this bottle I just bought?" And again the salesman replied, "No."

I then waited for a while; no one moved and so before leaving I said, "You are a wise guy, aren't you?" He never denied that he was a wise guy, in fact he shook his head as if to agree.

I want you to know that I drop in to your store

regularly to buy various products for my tape recorder. I no longer intend to do so because of the above incident. I feel the salesman (he was the one wearing a white shirt, black pants and shoes) acted in a nasty and impolite manner and I am angered by it. If a customer wishes to withhold his name and address, that is his perogative. The salesman certainly should NOT deny the customer the paper bag.

This store is a part of my neighborhood and until I hear word from you I will not only avoid recommending the store to others but I will repeat my experience to my fellow neighbors!

To a house-painting firm in Cleveland

Your company recently painted the house we occupy.

At the time I complained about the men urinating in a rusty tub in our basement which then leaked out. Last nite we discovered that they had also used our trash can to urinate in as well.

I am notifying the proper authorities (1) of the disgusting way the men used our basement (2) the damp touching of our personal things stored in the basement.

To the head office of a fast-food restaurant chain

Last Monday I was fired from my job as asst. manager at your restauranat #689. I was told by the head manager, Ms. Johnson, that I was fired for the following reasons:

1. Not able to follow working schedule that is made for me.
2. Careless where money is concern. When cashing out a crew person, if he is short, I don't count back-up bank to see if money is in it.
3. I bring my TV to work and sit in the manager's office and watch TV when I should be out on the floor making sure the crew members are doing what they are getting paid for.
4. When working at night and the store gets crowded with customers, I won't help out. I am afraid of getting dirty because I am going out after work.

I feel that these reasons are petty and personal, reasons made up by Ms. Johnson to get rid of me because she does not like me. I tried to explain to Ms. Johnson that these were petty and stupid reasons to fire me for, but she just can't be wrong. When I was a crew person, Ms. Johnson always liked me. Whenever she needed someone to work overtime or to come in early she would always call me. But after I got into management, she changed. She must have thought I was after her job. She would ask the other managers questions about me when I felt if she wanted to know anything about me, she should have asked me. I have never went out of my way to be naughty to Ms. Johnson or to give her a bad time.

What makes me angry is the fact that Ms. Johnson NEVER works at night nor was she working on the days that these reasons for firing me occurred, so how can she fire me for something that she doesn't know is true or false. In the past whenever there was a problem between crew and management or crew and crew Ms. Johnson would always call the parties involved together and they would discuss the problem. But with me she just FIRED ME—NO WARNING, NO HEARING, NO NOTHING.

To a manufacturer of greeting cards

I would like to bring to your attention a situation that my wife brought to mine. While shopping for a Valentine's Day card, she was a bit surprised to overhear another lady exclaim "Oh, no!" She soon learned the reason for the exclamation.

We think it is unnecessary that a company like yours lower its standards to such an extent that sexually oriented valentines be stocked on open shelves, if at all. The use of four-letter words, although found in the later dictionaries, seem to have no place in valentine cards, especially remembering the origin of the day. The type of sexual activities that some couples may wish to engage in are best left to the privacy of the bedroom, instead of being annotated for the education of children who may wish to purchase a greeting for their parents.

You obviously do not understand the disgust that these items arouse in the majority of shoppers.

To the head office of a supermarket chain

Please take notice that on the last two occasions, same being Monday and Tuesday of this current week, that I tried to buy food at your supermarket, the store did not have either of the two MEAT SPECIALS that it advertised, same being very reasonable beef, i.e. chuck steaks at 59¢ pound and hamburger at 79¢ pound in three or more pound quantities. The only beef displayed was expensive cut beef. There was ample budget priced chicken and the advertised chicken items and prices, thus manipulating me to use chicken.

My stomach swells terribly when I eat chicken. So this is to notify you that I intend to hold you criminally liable for lethal tool-use of me, targetting me in an effort to kill me with this synthetic product sold me as food.

To a department store in Los Angeles, from a lady who had previously written to register her exasperation with a malfunctioning sewing machine purchased at the store

Since you are *not* handling my problem with my sewing machine and instead I have to write to some man in New Jersey as you instructed me in your letter, I would like the *four* 13¢ stamps you so politely helped yourself to. I would also like to be reimbursed for the one 13¢ stamp it cost me to send you this letter. And if I don't get the stamps back, I'm coming down there *and it won't be pleasant.*

It's bad enough as it is today and you fucking crooks ask for *four* 13¢ stamps—you don't even say what you'll use them for—and then you don't even send them back to me—and you have the fucking nerve to take them and ask me to spend another 13¢ to send my problem to some New Jersey asshole who will probably just ask for more stamps for himself.

IV

Letters to Various Public Figures and Institutions, Alleging Misconduct by Others

To the editor of The Times, *London, 1905, from George Bernard Shaw*

The Opera management at Covent Garden regulates the dress of its male patrons. When is it going to do the same to the women?

On Saturday night I went to the Opera. I wore the costume imposed on me by the regulations of the house. I fully recognize the advantage of those regulations. Evening dress is cheap, simple, durable, prevents rivalry and extravagance on the part of male leaders of fashion, annihilates class distinctions, and gives men who are poor and doubtful of their social position (that is the great majority of men) a sense of security and satisfaction that no clothes of their own choosing could confer, besides saving a whole sex the trouble of considering what they should wear on state occasions. The objections to it are as dust in the balance in the eyes of the ordinary Briton. These objections are that it is colourless and characterless; that it involves a whitening process which makes the shirt troublesome, slightly uncomfortable, and seriously unclean; that it acts as a passport for undesirable persons; that it fails to guarantee sobriety, cleanliness, and order on the part of the wearer; and that it reduces to a formula a very vital human habit which should be the subject of constant experiment and active private enterprise. All such objections are thoroughly un-English. They appeal only to an eccentric few, and may be left out of account with the fantastic objections of men like Ruskin, Tennyson, Carlyle, and Morris to tall hats.

But I submit that what is sauce for the gander is sauce for the goose. Every argument that applies to the regulation of the man's dress applies equally to the regulation of the woman's. Now let me describe what actually happened to me at the Opera. Not only was I in evening dress by compulsion, but I voluntarily added many graces of conduct as to which the management made no stipulation whatever. I was in my seat in time for the first chord of the overture. I did not chatter during the music nor raise my voice when the Opera was too loud for normal conversation. I did not get up and go out when the statue music began.

My language was fairly moderate considering the number and nature of the improvements on Mozart volunteered by Signor Caruso, and the respectful ignorance of the dramatic points of the score exhibited by the conductor and the stage manager—if there is such a functionary at Covent Garden. In short, my behaviour was exemplary.

At 9 o'clock (the Opera began at 8) a lady came in and sat down very conspicuously in my line of sight. She remained there until the beginning of the last act. I do not complain of her coming late and going early; on the contrary, I wish she had come later and gone earlier. For this lady, who had very black hair, had stuck over her right ear the pitiable corpse of a large white bird, which looked exactly as if someone had killed it by stamping on its breast, and then nailed it to the lady's temple, which was presumably of sufficient solidity to bear the operation. I am not, I hope, a morbidly squeamish person, but the spectacle sickened me. I presume that if I had presented myself at the doors with a dead snake round my neck, a collection of blackbeetles pinned to my shirtfront, and a grouse in my hair, I should have been refused admission. Why, then is a woman to be allowed to commit such a public outrage? Had the lady been refused admission, as she should have been, she would have soundly rated the tradesman who imposed the disgusting headdress on her under the false pretence that 'the best people' wear such things, and withdrawn her custom from him; and thus the root of the evil would be struck at; for your fashionable woman generally allows herself to be dressed according to the taste of a person whom she would not let sit down in her presence. I once, in Drury Lane Theatre, sat behind a *matinee* hat decorated with the two wings of a seagull, artificially reddened at the joints so as to produce the illusion of being freshly plucked from a live bird. But even that lady stopped short of the whole seagull. Both ladies were evidently regarded by their neighbours as ridiculous and vulgar; but that is hardly enough when the offence is one which produces a sensation of physical sickness in persons of normal humane sensibility.

I suggest to the Covent Garden authorities that, if they feel bound to protect their subscribers against the danger of my shocking them with a blue tie, they are at least equally bound to protect me against the danger of a woman shocking me with a dead bird.

To the New York Police Department

Yesterday, at roughly 16:05 hours, despite my efforts to resist, I was manipulated and tricked into becoming trapped in a narrow check-out line at the supermarket on the corner.

I was trapped between an older Italian woman ahead of me who stalled the male cashier with a large denomination bill and an aggressive older Caucasian male behind me who had helped trick me into the narrow aisle. I was held prisoner for several minutes, I believe. I was greatly disturbed.

This has happened before. I want you to check out who is behind this.

To the editor of the New York Tribune, *from Thurlow Weed, a journalist with the* Albany Evening Journal, *after the novelist James Fenimore Cooper had been awarded $400 in an undefended libel suit against Weed*

This meagre verdict under the circumstances is a severe and mortifying rebuke to Cooper, who had everything his own way. The value of Mr. Cooper's character, therefore, has been judicially determined. It is worth exactly four hundred dollars.

To the American Bar Association

I am writing this letter to get something off my chest.

I have had two heart attacks in the last four years and my wife has had THREE MAJOR OPERATIONS IN THE LAST TWO YEARS therefore I have fallen behind on bills. So far I have not had any unpleasant feelings or words with any attorney except the attorney of whom I am writing about.

This attorney had a few bills turned over to him for collection and I started payments on them and as soon as I would get one almost paid up he would bring another one into Small Claims Court just to add up on the bills and to make it that much harder for me to catch up. This went along until May of 1964 then I received a summons to appear in Small Claims Court for a bill that I supposedly owed to a car dealer. On that date I was in the hospital with a Heart Attack so I wrote to the district court and informed them of this. They proceeded to postpone the case until I was able to appear then on November 10th I received a notice from this attorney that the case would come up on November 19th. I asked him to postpone it for a week and he refused. I was scheduled to work on the 19th that was why I wanted it postponed. I forgot that that would be Thanksgiving so I went to district court and they postponed the case till the 3rd of December that was one of my days off. So on the 3rd of December I appeared the case was called and I was told I was to get a hearing in a short while. Then this attorney called me out in the hall and told me he had a Judgment against me from the power and light company and another car dealer and he wanted to know what I was going to do about them. I informed him that I was completely paid up on both accounts and he informed me I was not. So luckily because I did not trust this attorney (and I informed him of this) I had brought along my cancelled checks signed by his office and I let him see them so he copied down the dates and asked me about some bills from a garage. I told him I did not owe them any money and he took out a couple of bills and one of them had my signature on it. I had forgotten about it. The bill was for aligning my sons car for $6.75. The bill was for $13.50 they had added the $6.75 twice so this attorney called the garage from a pay phone and they agreed to the bill being for $6.75. Then he had a bill for work done on a 1961 Falcon which was my daughter's car. By the way the summons read for repairs and labor on a 1956 Ford convertible! Anyway I agreed that if she had not paid the bill I would making the amount $16.60 plus $2.00 cost of courts. But I told him I would not be able to pay on the bill till the end of January and he said as long as I would agree to this it would be all right so he went in to the Clerk of Court and informed him that he had agreed on a $16.60 balance so evidently the court entered a Judgment against me for that amount. On the 23rd of January I received another notice to appear in court on the 4th of February for not having paid the Judgment that was made against me adding another 75¢ to the bill. Now you know that if I were to go before the judge on the 3rd of December he would of had to throw it all out except the $6.75 which was mine but that is not what I wanted. All I want to know is DO ALL LAWYERS SNEAK AROUND THIS WAY???

To Zsa Zsa Gabor and others, many others

I went to see "40 Carats" on Friday and was disappointed that you were not on stage. Someone said that your hair dresser did not show up, but the real reason was that a department of our government wanted me to have a disappointing night at the theatre and proceeded to have the management change my seat and to further harass me they arranged that you were not to appear.

This is not the first time they have gone to such extremes to impress me with their evil power. Seven years ago on radio station WOR, New York, "Long John Nebble" was fired because I was a regular listener to his program and Mr. Nebble would not allow unscheduled guests disrupt his program to send me unimportant messages in code.

By now you have guessed it; I am a government spy against my will. Our government has been teaching my children to be spys and I am helpless to stop them. There are many thousands of U.S. citizens in the same dilemma as I am.

I have a transistor in my tooth put there against my will by our government. I am a walking radio station; I send and receive voice impulses. In a word I am a robot; my thinking is controlled as well as the physical actions of my body. That is the reason I have taken refuge in a V.A. Hospital. I have tried to get a lawyer or have the transistor removed to no avail.

Someone needs to expose this to the American public. I leave it in your hands.

P.S. For 8 years they have been feeding me excessive amounts of "thorazine" to dull my thinking and tried desperately to turn me into an alcoholic and discredit me so I would not work against them. They had my wife divorce me without notifying me, then moved my family to Florida and I have only seen my children four times in 10 years. They had a social worker attempt to drive my wife to suicide after my wife had illegally divorced me so that I would marry a woman of their choosing.

At this writing they are trying to get my wife to marry again in hopes that it will make me want to get married. The reason they don't like my wife is that she has a deformity of the spine. Is it any wonder I smoke 3 and 4 packs of cigarettes a day. To further harass me they put a childrens show on TV with a chimpanzee with my name that had a transistor in its tooth. One of the first things they tested me for was to see if I would make a good pyromaniac. They wanted me to set fire to my house and collect the insurance. The rash of fires in the Atlantic City area around Oct., Nov. and Dec. of 1965 was in reprisal for me writing letters to Congressmen and Pres. Johnson. More persecution. If I'm wrong I'll eat your hat.

Copies sent to the following:

Long John Nebble
Barry Farber
F.B.I.
All U.S. Senators and Representatives
American Civil Liberties Union
All government agencies
Army, Navy, Marines, Coast Guard
President Nixon
President Johnson
Director, Veterans Administration
All 50 U.S. governors
Legal Aid Society
Better Business Bureau
Jack Anderson
Heads of churches and synagogues in U.S.

Fulton Lewis III
American Medical Association
Labor unions
ABC, NBC, CBS
United Press International
New York Times
Attorney General of each state in U.S.
U.S. Attorney General
American Legion
Veterans of Foreign Wars
Disabled American Veterans
Democratic National Committee
Republican National Committee
League of Women Voters in all 50 states
Woodrow Wilson School of Government, Princeton, N.J.
Dean of Yale Law School
Philip and Daniel Berrigan
Martha Mitchell
Ralph Nader
National Council of Churches
George Romney
Jesse Unruh
Jimmy the Greek
Colleges of Medicine and Dentistry
Vice-President Agnew
Sargent Shriver
Mayors of all major cities in U.S.
Secret Service
I.R.S.
Major industry in U.S.
F.A.A.
Bobby Seale
Ramsey Clark
N.A.A.C.P.
Federal Reserve Chairman
Draft Director
Boy Scouts of America
Y.M.C.A.
All airlines
General Motors
Ford
Chrysler
American Motors
I.T.T.
etc.

To the editor of The Times, *London, 1915*

A little light might be shed, with advantage, upon the high-handed methods of the Passports Department at the Foreign Office. On the form provided for the purpose I described my face as "intelligent." Instead of finding this characterization entered, I have received a passport on which some official utterly unknown to me, has taken it upon himself to call my face "oval."

To Senator Thomas H. Kuchel of California, following news stories concerning joint U.S. Army and NATO counter-insurgency exercises being held in Georgia

I am writing you in protest to the presence of foreign troops on American soil. That there are African Negro troops, who are cannables, stationed in Georgia!

The news has just broken, although there had been rumors for a week or more, that Georgia is the place for 16,000 African soldiers, being trained by the U.N. for guerilla warfare. Complete with nose and ear rings. This time, the U.N., and our State Department, have gone too far.

To the American Civil Liberties Union, from a man whose baroque letterhead identified him as a "Casual Laborer, Non-Residential Windows Washed, 10¢ per minute, Cash, No Estimates, No Promises, No Contracts, No Tips"

After reaching an agreement with the proprietor of a grocery store in East Harlem regarding the rate of compensation (10¢ per minute) I washed the outside and part of the inside of the store windows from 1:11 p.m. to 1:58 p.m. last Wednesday.

Although the glass surface area was not unduly great, access to the glass was impaired by roll-down overhead shutters, vertical bars inside the doors, neon signs, and cramped inside work areas. In addition, paint and other residue on the glass required removal by razor blade. All this increases the time involved and, therefore, the cost.

One or two minutes before I completed the job the proprietor commenced to "rag" me, in Jewish fashion, inquiring how much would it cost.

Although the work took 47 minutes, it is my present, temporary, unannounced practice to give an automatic 10% discount on work of 30 minutes or more (20% discount on 60 minutes; 30% discount on 120 minutes). Thus, I presented the proprietor with a bill for $4.20.

He protested that this was too much money and offered $3.00 instead. I insisted upon $4.20 until his actions indicated that he intended to come from behind the counter and resort to violence, whereupon I gathered up my possessions and left the premises, leaving the $3.00 on the counter.

While I was bent over my bucket at the curb the proprietor's accomplice approached with four $1.00 bills that I rejected. I yelled at a passing police car, but it disappeared in the distance. Then the proprietor's accomplice reappeared and paid me with four $1.00 bills and two dimes. (One of the bills appeared to be strangely and uniformly moist or damp.) Then, another police car, apparently in response to a radio call from the earlier police car, pulled up to the curb. I explained to the officer that I had been given a bad time about my charge for window washing, but that I had been paid, and that everything was all right.

If the proprietor is not a genuine "dead-beat," then perhaps he is a police "stake-out," or a member of some other authoritarian social control group that wants to make trouble for me in that particular neighborhood. Either way the community should be alerted to the situation. If they are doing these things to me, they are probably doing the same things to other citizens on an assembly-line basis.

To the Better Business Bureau

Recently I made a trip to New York City and I was ripped off at the Empire State Bldg. On Tuesday, April 26th, I purchased a ticket. It was a rainy day. On the ground however you could see quite a distance and I thought visibility was good enouf. When I bought the ticket the indicator by the ticket counter read "0–2 miles." The woman there did not say anything about the visibility.

When I got to the top you couldn't see anything. There was zero visibility. I immediately knew I'd been ripped off.

I went back down and complained. The woman said, "Look, the sign says 'no visibility'." I said that when I bought the ticket it had read "0–2 miles." I asked to talk to the manager.

The manager happened to be right there, When I told him my complaint—that I'd paid $1.75 to see nothing—he was immediately hostile. I couldn't see his reasoning. He said I was told at the time I bought the ticket that there was no visibility. I told him I thought I should get a refund, that I sure didn't pay the money to ride an elevator to the top. He still said I could get no refund.

After the manager, who was hostile the entire time and who blamed me for not knowing there wasn't any visibility, had again refused me a refund I called him an "asshole". He then became very angry and yelled in my face, "Don't you ever call me that" and called the "security". I left then, ripped off of the $1.75. I feel that I'm entitled to a refund of the money.

This is to report the sharp practices of the shoe repair shop across the street.

Upon delivery, today, of a pair of regular man's shoes with a specific request for Cat's Paw Brand rubber heels, I was promised Cat's Paw heels, and I was asked to pay in advance.

When I returned for the shoes, other rubber heels had been attached, inferior in quality and half the thickness. The proprietors said they had no Cat's Paw heels, with a shelf full of Cat's Paw heels staring down at them.

I insist that one of your people bring in a pair of regular shoes and try the same thing. See what happens.

Why do tenants have to pay rent to park cars outside with ice on grounds and danger of other cars skidding and crashing into them?

After plow is used the old people have to shovel snow away from garage doors in order to get car out. They cant get car in garage due to ice and all night there is yelling of men trying to push cars around and I dont blame them but the neighbors have to suffer due to a neglectful and selfish landlord.

These men are late for work and can get rupture in pushing cars around.

Concerning the ABC Charm School Director, Miss Josephine Follette—Where does this woman get the nerve to claim she is an expert in teaching modeling, etc. She claims thru an article in the newspapers and at classes that she is a fashion reporter, top model, and a graduate of the "New York Success School." I have made enquiries and find that their is no such school as "New York Success School" and never has been. This woman dupes and makes money on the good will of others.

PAYOLA—TELEVISION QUIZZES—CHEATS—CHEATS—CHEATS.

I want to make a complaint about a nursery. I have been "gypped" by this firm.

Last year I went there with my son-in-law and daughter specially to pick out a special plant for Mother's Day. I requested a red-orange Talisman Rose with yellow center. I have none like it in my garden, but have what I call "junk bushes" many of these all over, and didn't need what *they* sold me for $4.95. These junky rosebushes are thorny all over, a nuisance nobody wants, as they grow "wild" and I have more of those wild things than I want.

This "Talisman" they sold me—they told me to bury the whole thing, which I did, per their instructions. The way that this phoney company operates is—the tag they put on the bush is on the bottom and gets buried and rots in the ground, so you have no evidence; and they say "No receipt, no tag?" Now they have put up by their cash register a new sign that there are No Guarantees on anything they sell.

Well, the bush turned out to be one of those "junk" white wild rosebushes, full of giant thorns. I had planted this bush where everyone would see the pretty rosebush, according to their picture—on the front corner of my house, in a small area. A monster grew up. Monstrous white wild rosebush instead of Talisman. They had cheated me and say, always, when you make a purchase, if not satisfied, bring it back, and then don't make good on their foul deal. If you say you'll dig it up, they say, We don't want it, it's not our fault.

I have also lost more than $30 with this nursery on the large "clay" pot. The old man who runs the place lies all the time, to cover up, and when you demand action, he walks away to avoid you. He pretends, for one thing, and many believe him, that *he* is not the boss. I had many bad experiences with this man. I don't know what to do, but wanted to call the police the last time he cheated me. He said "Go ahead, I won't do *any*thing—I'm sorry!" He wasn't "sorry." I said you're not sorry, you're happy you got my $30 and now you won't make good on the large heavy flowerpot that is falling apart into sand all over my rug and into my hands. This old man talked me into buying this very large heavy pot for my two difenbachias and it is so heavy I can't lift it, once you get the dirt in it, and even though I would bring it back, they are not making good their sales.

It is this company's custom to keep quiet, no one opens their mouths, they are afraid of their jobs I guess —so it is a wasted trip over there every time. They just don't make good their sales like other stores—the only thing they are interested in is taking your money.

On April 19th I was taken to the hospital by Police Ambulance. After examination, I was put into the Coronary Care Unit for three days (and all the time I was *scared*, and I mean *scared*, having all kinds of tests, cardiograms, etc., etc., etc.).

Then I was put into this ward, for the remainder of my stay, until April 30th. This included more and more tests, etc., etc., etc., and all the time I was *scared*. They sent me home, with medication and diet. The doctors said that my blood pressure was *very high*.

At the time of my stay at the hospital, I received literature from a company asking me to send them $74.79 for a memorial marker. I have never heard of anything like this in my life—and people that I have spoken to just *looked* at me and said the same thing!

Something should be done about such advertising—especially when people are in the hospital.

There is a man selling week old Sunday papers on Saturday night in front of the Waldorf Restaurant on the upper part of Main Street. I have bought his papers. He should be put out of business.

My inquiry is solely and specifically as follows: Does any restaurant (defined as a public eating place) have the right to legally refuse, at any time of the day, to serve you certain food items (which are shown on their order and menu boards)? Using the "excuse," as they say, "we are not serving breakfast any more this morning." In as much as this took place well within what the average person considers breakfast time (10 A.M.), hence this letter.

My reasoning for being told such an absurd statement is I believed that any public restaurant, with the food in stock, sort of had to serve what was ordered. After all, anyone can eat what they want, and so therefore who can say I can't be served bacon and eggs, etc. at 7 P.M. to midnight, or have steak and potatoes, for what is deemed breakfast time?

Who is, or, who does, define, and decide, what constitutes what I, or 1,000 other people, can *get* for any specific mealtime? Of course this is done simply to manipulate the store prices to their liking. On leaving, I told the employee, then why don't you take down the sign? Of course, I was given an argument.

I want your reaction to a situation that has been developed over the past decade or two which works a hardship upon every person affected with various impediments, such as Arthritis, Broken Limbs, Stiff Knees, Heavy Bodies, and recovery from sickness (weakness). I refer to the prevailing installation of low (and I mean LOW) toilet seats. They are not only hard to sit down on but HARDER to get up from. I am speaking from experiance. I expect a reply from you.

I would like to complain about this Department Store.

They have a security guard following you around the street harrassing people, telling people to watch out for that person, because she is a thief and a pick pocker. This has been going on for two years now, and it is time for it to stop. One day I stop and ask the person why are they doing this. They told me the Department Store told them to do this. I saw the person working for the Department Store two years ago as a security guard. This man has been harrassing me ever since. He calls me on the phone calls me names like thief and pick pocker. This has been going on for two years, and I am getting sick of this. He is telling people to look at that thief and pick pocker. I asked him one day who told him to do that he said the Department Store.

If this store is the kind of store to harrass people for two years, they don't need to be in business. And who needs Security like that. I have not been in the store in two years. I cannot walk down the street and go into a store for them saying look at that thief and pick pocker.

I am not a thief or pick pocker. People don't have anything else to do with themself.

V

Letters on the Delicate Subject of Money

To a gentleman who had acted dishonorably in a financial matter, from Cornelius Vanderbilt

You have undertaken to cheat me. I will not sue you because the law takes too long. I will ruin you.

To a debtor, 1824, who was tardy in paying his bill

A severe pressure in pecuniary matters compels me to address you in a manner which may not perhaps be pleasing.

The sum you are indebted to me ought, in justice, to have been paid six months since, from which period you have constantly trifled with me, by offering trivial excuses.

You must be aware that I cannot possibly carry on

my business, and pay my creditors punctually, unless regular returns are made to me; and I have only to add, that unless you send me a remittance, I must (however reluctantly I may do it) pursue other means for the recovery of my due.

I shall conclude, sir, by recommending you, if you are anxious to prosper, to be diligent in your business, and, above all things, to be punctual in the payment of your bills.

To a tradesman, 1806, who had requested a postponement of the repayment date on a loan

Having paid the note away previous to the receipt of your letter, I do not possess the power of complying with your request. You must, therefore, prepare to take it up when due, or your character will suffer.

To a literary agent in New York, from an impecunious author who had grown impatient at not receiving royalty payments that were due him

Look, I'll give you fifty percent—that's 50%, in case your literacy is still lagging behind your numeracy—

look, I'll give the United Jewish Appeal fifty percent —sorry, 50%—I'll give *anybody* 50%—that's *half*—of *anything* you can squeeze out of those sphincters.

Just do it soon. I'm tired of waiting.

Otherwise next week I'm taking the true story of my indentured serfdom to every trade paper and association and gossip sheet here and in Europe onward and upward until vengeance is mine, mine, all mine.

If you can get that message through their sloping Simian foreheads, good. If not, the avenging angel of retribution will verily smite them with the biggest fucking non-kosher pickle ever to splatter their engorged membranes.

So you're in a rare position to help them/me/yourself. All you have to do is tease a few shekels out of their sclerotic, knotted, hairy, translucent, warty, mucous-spotted, semen-coated, cologne-scented, white-knuckled fists. And I'll be happy.

But you've only got one week to do it in. That's all. One. (Sorry, 1.) Then I'm going to rip out their diseased, bacteria-ravaged spleens and their spongy, shriveled prostate glands and stuff them up their gaping Levantine nostrils and douse their festering, scab-encrusted bodies with the finest high-octane fuel and light their little circumcised fuses and watch their mottled flesh crackle and bubble from pink to yellow to brown.

Then I'm going to piss on the fire.

To the Hertfordshire (England) County Council, from a religious education teacher who had been informed that his salary would be delayed

I trust by now you have the forms you requested and I am writing to ask that you act upon them as quickly as possible. I was not informed until the 29th September—in other words, until I had been teaching for four weeks—that I was not to be paid at the same time as the rest of the staff, and had in consequence arranged for various bills to fall due at that time. As a result of this financial bombshell, I am heavily in debt to my bank—I have been prevented from writing any more cheques, for the first time in my financial career; I am behind with the rent, and owe telephone, gas and electricity bills. My savings are exhausted, and I have already borrowed £60 from my school.

Fortunately I have only temporarily moved my furniture, and only temporarily paid for my petrol. I have found a snug alleyway to sleep in, live quite comfortably off grubs and roots, and have even learned to weave spiders' webs in faery fashion into a passable pair of socks. However, the time is rapidly approaching when I shall find real money to be a help—especially as my local Tesco's has refused to accept any more buttons—and, as I have been employed in some way by Hertfordshire for six weeks now, I look to you to provide the same, and set my mind at rest.

I am well aware that "the love of money is the root

of all evil" (I Tim. 6.10); however, I would remind you that "the labourer is worthy of his hire," and would refer you to Leviticus 19, verse 13: "The wages of a hired servant shall not remain with you all night until the morning." I realise that the wages of sin are death (Rom. 6.23), but had hoped that those for teaching might be a little more palatable.

It is possible that, as a newcomer, I have not fully understood the nuances of salary slips etc.—but "when a stranger sojourns with you in your land, you shall not do him wrong; the stranger who sojourns with you shall be to you as a native among you" (Lev. 19.33). "And if your brother becomes poor, and cannot maintain himself with you, you shall maintain him" (Lev. 25.35).

I await your cheque with great interest, compounded at 2½% per week.

To the Pennsylvania Department of Public Assistance

I am writing to say that my baby was born two years old. When do I get my money?

I am very annoyed that you have branded my son illiterate. This is a dirty lie, as I was married a week before he was born.

My husband got his project cut off two weeks ago, and I haven't had any relief since.

I cannot get sick pay. I have six children. Can you tell me why?

This is my eighth child. What are you going to do about it?

Unless I get my husbands money pretty soon, I will be forced to lead an immortal life.

To a New York publisher, from an English author who considered the publisher unnecessarily dilatory in fulfilling his contractual obligations

1. According to the terms of a contract dated November 15, 1974, your company purchased the American rights in a certain book. Also according to these terms, your company agreed to pay the author "$1,000 on signing of the contract." As of May 9, 1975, however, this modest sum had somehow still not been paid to the author. What is your explanation for this curious situation?

   (a) We are slowly going bankrupt and we like to keep it that way: slowly
   (b) We are not going bankrupt but we would be if we were to start taking seriously every silly little clause in every contract we sign
   (c) It is not the easy way or the popular way, but it is the right way
   (d) We wanted to pay you but our treasurer embezzled the money
   (e) We did pay you but your agent embezzled the money
2. What do you propose to do to rectify this situation?
   (a) Take the limited hang-out route
   (b) Contact our bank in Mexico
   (c) Try a little benign neglect
   (d) Your check's in the mail
   (e) I don't understand the question
3. In view of the fact that six months is a rather long time in which to try to scrape up $1,000, what will be your response to the inevitable, scurrilous rumors that your company is in a financial hole of truly awesome dimensions?
   (a) We can see the light at the end of the tunnel
   (b) We can see the tunnel
   (c) Hello out there
   (d) Nolo contendere
   (e) I was only following orders
4. Having signed the above-mentioned contract as a witness, do you frequently find yourself in the position of having to witness atrocities on behalf of the firm?

(a) Every day
(b) Every other day
(c) It would be wrong, that's for sure
(d) I can't remember
(e) Wait for me behind the door marked "Showers"

5. As you know, an unusual emigré agent negotiated this contract. What is your opinion of her?
   (a) She is a very warm and wonderful human being
   (b) She is a mother
   (c) She is no more of a pain in the ass than all the other lousy agents in this stinking town who think they can bleed us for every last cent but, boy, have they got another think coming
   (d) It is my understanding that certain parties have contacted the Immigration & Naturalization Service about the possibility of her deportation on the basis of a number of serious allegations and therefore I think I should refrain from commenting on her case until it has been disposed of through the proper channels
   (e) Compared to what?
6. How do you view your own future in publishing? I intend to keep
   (a) calm
   (b) the faith
   (c) the home fires burning
   (d) hanging in there
   (e) up the good work
   (f) a low profile

(g) on truckin'
(h) out of trouble
(i) apologizing for my boss

To a creditor, 1815, who had refused a request for extra time in the settlement of a bill, and in so doing had taken the opportunity to deliver a short sermon on fiscal responsibility

The advice, which your letter of yesterday contains, is so *pithy*, so *laconic*, and so *much to the purpose*, that it cannot fail to have its due weight with myself. But after an acquaintance of many years, during which period some hundreds of dollars have been paid by me to you, and with the utmost regularity, I little expected the *lecturing* you have been pleased to favour me with; but you may depend on it, sir, I shall never again place it in your power to *school* me as to the mode in which I should conduct my business. I am only sorry that I have laid you under the necessity of refusing so trifling a favour. I beg, therefore, to inform you that, through the kindness of a friend, I shall be enabled, on this day week, not only to satisfy the demand you make, but also, at the same time, to settle the balance which will then be due to you. If, therefore, you will either send a receipt, or call yourself, on that day, the account shall be closed, and all correspondence between us on that, or any other subject, ended.

To a creditor who had rather aggressively demanded repayment of a loan, from an undertaker

As you well know, I have been unable to pay you because business has been slow. Why don't you help my business and drop dead?

To a mail-order firm in Connecticut

Please ask the creatures in your back room to discontinue sending statements to us.

My wife and I have NO merchandise received from your outfit and we owe you NO money.

The inclosed complete statement received today is comparable to the previous statements we have received from your gang.

Please note that the inclosed mass produced unsigned letter is not dated which procedures we have found to be typical of the harassment conducted by the SUB-human members of the Roman Catholic Idol Worshippers Sect.

To Professor R.M. Dawkins, from Frederick William Rolfe (Baron Corvo), 1910, after Dawkins had written the chronically impoverished author to complain of his relentless hostility and ingratitude whenever anyone tried to render him financial assistance

I don't for the life of me know what to say to yours of the 24th ult. My pneumonia, caused by walking about frosty nights on the Lido shore last March, has done me more harm than I thought. And I have had an unspeakably awful time these last 21 months, which shows no sign of lifting. My difficulty is that I can't imagine a way of writing to you without offence, AND without seeming to ask for your friendship and your money, both of which I want, but will not touch—with tongs—unless voluntarily and spontaneously pressed on me. . . .

Do you wonder that I was, and am, in a blazing rage with all of you, who, with roofs above your heads and beds to sleep in and regular meals, could desert me and leave me to the horribly offensive torments which naturally fell to me—could, in your circumstances, pit yourself against me, in mine. . . .

Autumn 1909, and winter, I lived on the open landing of a servant's stair, chopping and carrying firewood and doing a fattorini's job. And I managed to write another book. This I offered to assign to Barbieri (to the amount of my debt) if he'd give me any sort of refuge where I could work. The sneers and insults I endure are indescribable. I live in a dark den on the floor of the narrow side-alley, where no sun has ever been, where I have trapped 61 rats since June, served after servants, and without a soul to speak to, and with clothes unchanged since August 1908. And so on. But you act, not in cold blood, but in anger. Oh, my God! Hostile? No: I am not hostile to anyone who has not robbed me of my work, of my means of living, of my tools of trade. Olive-branch? No: if I offer olive-branches, I label myself as a conquered coward, a sucker-up, a toad-eater, the potential spunger you think me. It's no good writing any more. I shall never make you understand. You had a chance of making an equal and a friend. And you threw it away. We were both losers. But I'm the one who suffered.

To a philatelic society in Australia, when it persisted in demanding from a customer payments which had already been made

I am intensely dissatisfied with your organization and shall recommend it to the Russians as a prime nuclear target.

You are confused as to what the problem is. Let me explain while I have some workable sanity left:

1. I receive a set of covers in due order.
2. I send off my payment in due order.
3. 60 to 90 days later I get a past due notice.

4. I panic.
5. I check my records and find that I have paid in due order and therefore your notice is all wrong.
6. This has happened with *every* issue since May '77.
7. I gnash my teeth, pull my hair and rend my garments.
8. I complain but nobody listens.

Now I find that I have received and paid for 25 sets or $125 worth. Set #25 is not accounted for in your letter . . . but I sent you payment for that one way back in ancient times, so you should have record of it, but I just have the absolute feeling that I will soon be receiving a past due notice for it.

I have no choice therefore but to visit upon you my own particularly divine wrath and CANCEL MY SUBSCRIPTION.

To an oil company, after it had declined to reinstate a customer's credit card until he had paid the amount outstanding on his expired card and had filled out a new application

This is all a big *lie*. I did not use my credit card in 4 years, then too your company would have billed me. I last paid my bill back in 1972. Now you're trying to give me a lot of "Redirect" and loud talk *gimmickery*.

And I'm not going for your *Garbage-Talk.* So just send me, like I said, a new Credit Card, cause I'm not filling out your application again, you have one already! So, back to the drawing-board just like all those government hand-outs that your company gave to those officials in Washington.

To a creditor who had resorted to severe language in requesting payment of a sum seriously overdue, from a British naval officer, 19th century

I am in receipt of your "Final Demand" for payment of my account. I have to inform you that my normal practice concerning the settlement of debts is to place all of my bills in a hat once a month, from which I draw out two or three for payment. I have followed this procedure with regard to your bill. However, if I receive another letter from you, Sir, the tone of which I consider to be rude, your bill will not be put in the hat at all.

VI

Letters to People Who Have Behaved or Corresponded in an Especially Annoying Manner

To James Macpherson, an author, from Samuel Johnson, in reply to a threatening letter from the author, whose book Dr. Johnson had described as utterly without merit

I received your foolish and impudent letter. Any violence offered me I shall do my best to repel; and what I cannot do for myself, the law shall do for me. I hope I shall never be deterred from detecting what I think a cheat, by the menaces of a ruffian.

What would you have me retract? I thought your book an imposture; I think it an imposture still. For this opinion I have given my reasons to the publick, which I here dare you to refute. Your rage I defy. Your abilities, since your Homer, are not so formidable; and what I hear of your morals inclines me to pay regard not to what you shall say, but to what you shall prove.

To a gentleman of modest means and background, 1821, from a wealthy lady, in reply to an offer of marriage

I certainly was considerably surprised at the receipt of your letter, containing an offer of your hand. Surely, sir, you must have been labouring under some degree of mental derangement when you wrote it, otherwise you could not have the presumption to hope for a return of love from a person so greatly your superior as I am.

Wishing you to consider this reply as a positive rejection of your suit, I trust you will not address any future letters to me; if you do, I shall be under the painful necessity of returning them unopened.

To Richard Meltzer, rock music critic, after he had responded to an unpleasant letter by sending his correspondent a box of chocolates extensively pre-infested with insects of the family Blattidae

Thanx a lot you fucking shithead the goddam cockroaches escaped as soon as I opened the goddam bonbon box, & them other things moved into my short hairs & the free clinic says all my children will be born dead (in which case I'll send them to you for your Tropicana stillborn collection) or else they'll all be blind and have big heads which is actually cool because now I have a good excuse not to have kids running around the fucking house bothering me however I now have 62,100,000 cockroaches in the house and my roommate who's mexican & therefore has a congenital fear of cockroaches will never forgive me & is thinking of farmlaboring his way across the country to personally shove several cockroaches up your fucking bunz to eat you up from the inside if syphilis don't beat him to it.

As a token of my esteem please find one small meal enclosed, that was pre-chewed for you by a dead iguana we keep around the house for when we get horny & are too out of it or lazy or whatever to step down the blvd for one of those nice hollywood high teenie-bop hippieettes.

To John Ruskin, the 19th-century English art critic, after he had attempted to mitigate his vigorous condemnation of a friend's painting with the pronouncement that his views should not, of course, be allowed to interfere with their friendship

Ruskin—Next time I meet you I shall knock you down, but I hope it will make no difference in our friendship.

To W.S. Gilbert, English playwright and collaborator of the composer Arthur Sullivan in the composition of many popular operettas, after he had notified the Comtesse de Brémont that in order for him to agree to her request for an interview she would be required to pay the sum of twenty guineas

The Comtesse de Brémont presents her compliments to Mr. W.S. Gilbert and in reply to his answer to her request for an interview for *St Paul's* in which he states his terms as twenty guineas for that privilege, begs to say that she anticipates the pleasure of writing his obituary for nothing.

To a customer of a clothing store in Minneapolis, from the proprietor of the store, after the customer had written demanding a refund on a pair of trousers that had disintegrated within three weeks of purchase

Look you little turd, you write an ass-hole letter like the one you wrote here and expect to get results and you have to be out of your mind. I want you to know that I am really sorry to hear about your problems and if you presented them in a civilized letter I would be more than happy to refund your money. But you, you fucking idiot, you write and threaten my business, that's really smart.

Call your friends and tell them your heartaches, then after you've fumed and steamed for a day or so THINK.

When you're a little more grown up maybe we can do business.

To an upstairs neighbor, regarding his use of the plumbing

I very much regret having to complain, but we are frequently disturbed at a very early hour (5 a.m. this morning) and very late at night, by the indiscreet use of your toilets.

The plumbing in this building is very poor and if not used discreetly the tenants below are always aware of the toilets being used, and this coupled with pulling the chain late at night or early morning, is most disturbing and also embarrassing.

To the promoter of a concert in London featuring George Melly, English writer, musician, and singer, who has achieved a certain notoriety for his frequently vivid use of the language

At the concert with George Melly and John Chiltons Feetwarmers myself and many others were very disappointed with the continual bad language of George Melly. This made several people walk out of the Theatre. Certain words that were used to tell us about the songs, and words in the songs were nasty and uncalled for. His smutty act I do feel should have been adjusted from this type of language, not only because of children in the audience but also most women do not like these words.

To George Melly

George Melly your a repulsive sweaty faced lout singing love songs. Why your past it. Hang your gun up. And all your dirty jokes leave them to the real comediens. You have a mouth like a ducks ass. Have you only one suit and shabby at that. And your dirty sugestive songs. Somebody ought to tell you. You dirty minded oaf.

Your a load of rubbish.

To Michelangelo, from a friend who had wearied of the artist's consistently low opinion of others

The Pope, the Cardinal, and Jacopo Salviati are men who when they say yes, it is a written contract, inasmuch as they are true to their word, and not what you pretend them to be. You measure them with your own rod; for neither contracts nor plighted troth avail with you, who are always saying nay and yea according as you think it profitable.

In what concerns you, I have done all I could to promote your interests and honor, not having earlier perceived that you never conferred a benefit on anyone, and that, beginning with myself, to expect kindness from you would be the same as wanting water not to be wet. I have reason for what I say, since we have often met together in familiar converse, and may the day be cursed on which you ever said any good about anybody on earth.

To Upton Sinclair, who had recently lost an election for public office in California, from H.L. Mencken

According to news items reaching the East, you were lately running for something or other again. The people of California, it appears, turned you down, along with your brother messiah, Dr. Townsend. With the utmost friendliness, I can only say that I think they showed sound judgment. They have had plenty of chance to estimate both you and Townsend, and they prefer anybody else, including even Hoover. They refused to follow you as a Socialist, they refused to follow you as a

Prohibitionist, they refused to follow you as an electronic vibrator, they refused to follow you as a thought transferer, they refused to follow you as a Democrat, and now they refuse to follow you as anything whatsoever. The rule is that three strikes are out. To the bench, Comrade; to the bench!

To Ezra Pound, from H.L. Mencken, after he had been treated to a lengthy and typically quirky harangue on economics and politics

You are something behind-hand with that tirade, but if you want to print it I surely have no objection. Everything you say has been said before, first by the war patriots, then by the Ku Kluxers, then by the Anti-Saloon League brethren, then by the Harding visionaries, then by the Coolidge ditto, then by the apostles of Hoover's New Economy, and now by the New Dealers and Union Square Communists, with applause all along the line by the Single Taxers, chiropractors, anti-vivisectionists, surrealists, anti-Darwinians, Rotarians, Kiwanians, thought-transferers, Fundamentalists, Douglasites, pacifists, New Thoughters, one-crop farmers, American Legionnaires, osteopaths, Christian scientists, labor skates, and kept idealists of the *New Republic*.

In brief, you come to the defense of quackery too late. All you say or can say has been said 10,000 times before, and by better men. I say better men because there is plainly a quantitative if not a qualitative difference between quackeries, and hence between the gullibility of their customers. Thus, the imbecility of the Townsend Plan is appreciably less obvious than that of the Douglas Plan. Indeed, it must appear to every man not afflicted by the believing neurosis that there is more sense in even T.S. Eliot's surrender to High Church Episcopalianism than there is in your succumbing to the Douglas rumble-bumble.

You made your great mistake when you abandoned the poetry business, and set up shop as a wizard in general practise. You wrote, in your day, some very good verse, and I had the pleasure, along with other literary buzzards, of calling attention to it at the time. But when you fell into the hands of those London logrollers, and began to wander through pink fogs with them, all your native common sense oozed out of you, and you set up a caterwauling for all sorts of brummagem Utopias, at first in the aesthetic region only but later in the regions of political and aesthetic baloney. Thus a competent poet was spoiled to make a tin-horn politician.

Your acquaintance with actual politics, and especially with American politics, seems to be pathetically meagre. You write as if you read nothing save the *New Masses*. Very little real news seems to penetrate to Rapallo. Why not remove those obscene and archaic whiskers, shake off all the other stigmata of the Left Bank, come home to the Republic, and let me show you the greatest show on earth? If, after six months of it, you continue to believe in sorcery, whether poetical, political or economic, I promise to have you put to death in some painless manner, and to erect a bronze equestrian statue to your memory, alongside the one I am setting up in honor of Upton Sinclair.

Meanwhile, please don't try to alarm a poor old man by yelling at him and making faces. It has been tried before.

To General George B. McClellan, from President Abraham Lincoln, who during the course of the Civil War had become increasingly exasperated by the general's reluctance to send his troops into battle

If you don't want to use the army I should like to borrow it for a while.

To General McClellan, again

I have just read your dispatch about sore-tongued and fatigued horses. Will you pardon me for asking what the horses of your army have done since the battle of Antietam that fatigues anything?

To Abraham Lincoln, whose presence in the White House seemed to stir strange passions in citizens who disagreed with him

God damn your god damned old hellfired god damned soul to hell god damn you and god damn your god damned family's god damned hellfired god damned soul to hell and good damnation god damn them and god damn your god damn friends to hell.

Deformed Sir, The Ugly Club in full meeting have elected you an honorary Member of the Hood-Favored Fraternity. Prince Harry was lean, Falstaff was fat, Thersities was hunchbacked, and Slowkenlergus was renowned for the eminent miscalculation which Nature had made in the length of the nose; but it remained for you to unite all species of deformity and stand forth the Prince of Ugly Fellows.

To Representative Stephen M. Young of Ohio, after he had announced his opposition to a proposed bonus for veterans of World War I

My dog left home when he heard I had voted for you.

To Samuel Goldwyn, from Will Rogers, upon being notified that Goldwyn wanted to change the title of the film Jubilo

(VIA WESTERN UNION)

THOUGHT I WAS SUPPOSED TO BE A COMEDIAN BUT WHEN YOU SUGGEST CHANGING THE TITLE OF "JUBILO" YOU ARE FUNNIER THAN I EVER WAS. I DON'T SEE HOW LORIMER OF THE POST EVER LET IT BE PUBLISHED UNDER THAT TITLE. THAT SONG IS BETTER KNOWN THROUGH THE SOUTH BY OLDER PEOPLE THAN GERALDINE FARRAR'S HUSBAND. WE HAVE USED IT ALL THROUGH BUSINESS IN THE PICTURE BUT OF COURSE WE CAN CHANGE THAT TO "EVERYBODY SHIMMY NOW." SUPPOSE IF YOU HAD PRODUCED "THE MIRACLE MAN" YOU WOULD HAVE CALLED IT "A QUEER OLD GUY." BUT IF YOU REALLY WANT A TITLE FOR THIS SECOND PICTURE I WOULD SUGGEST "JUBILO." ALSO THE FOLLOWING:
"A POOR BUT HONEST TRAMP"
"HE LIES BUT HE DON'T MEAN IT"
"A FARMER'S VIRTUOUS DAUGHTER"
"THE GREAT TRAIN ROBBERY MYSTERY"
"A SPOTTED HORSE BUT HE IS ONLY PAINTED"
"A HUNGRY TRAMP'S REVENGE"
"THE VAGABOND WITH A HEART AS BIG AS HIS APPETITE"
"HE LOSES IN THE FIRST REEL BUT WINS IN THE LAST"

"THE OLD MAN LEFT BUT THE TRAMP PROTECTED HER" WHAT WOULD YOU HAVE CALLED "THE BIRTH OF A NATION"?

To a prodigal son, 1830, whose dissolute behavior had greatly displeased his father

William, I am truly grieved to find that all my remonstrances have been thrown away upon you, and that the advice I have given to you continues to be treated with contempt. It therefore becomes my solemn though melancholy duty to act with determination. I am resolved to do so, and no entreaties shall prevent me from resorting to every mode of punishment remaining in my power, unless you make an immediate reformation in your conduct.

In pursuance of this plan, I have given my agents a positive order never to advance you a single shilling on my account; and when your money is gone, young man, you will also then discover your real friends, though I greatly fear you have not one in the universe, with the exception of your injured and insulted father, who is yet even anxious to save you from utter destruction.

I have only to add, that should you still continue to persist in your present debauched line of conduct, I will for ever close my doors against you, and never exchange either a letter or syllable with you whilst I live.

To Lord Alfred Douglas, the very good friend of Oscar Wilde, from his father, the Marquis of Queensberry

Firstly, am I to understand that having left Oxford as you did, with discredit to yourself, the reasons of which were fully explained to me by your tutor, you now intend to loaf and loll about and do nothing? . . . I utterly decline, however, to just supply you with sufficient funds to enable you to loaf about. You are preparing a wretched future for yourself, and it would be most cruel and wrong for me to encourage you in this. Secondly, I come to the more painful part of this letter —your intimacy with this man Wilde. It must either cease or I will disown you and stop all money supplies. I am not going to try and analyze this intimacy, and I make no charge; but to my mind to pose as a thing is as bad as to be it. With my own eyes I saw you both in the most loathsome and disgusting relationship. . . .

(EDITOR'S NOTE: Lord Alfred replied, "You funny little man.")

To Mrs. Robert Sherwood, whose giving birth mercifully ended nine months of commentary on her pregnancy, from Dorothy Parker

(VIA WESTERN UNION)

WE ALL KNEW YOU HAD IT IN YOU.

To the Reverend Martin Luther King, Jr., from an anonymous "Negro," later revealed to be an FBI agent writing with the approval of J. Edgar Hoover

King, look into your heart. You know you're a complete fraud and a great liability to all of us Negroes. King, like all frauds, your end is approaching. You are done. Your Nobel Prize will not save you. The church organizations that have been helping—Protestant, Catholic and Jews—will know you for what you are—an evil, abnormal beast. King, there is only one thing left for you to do. You know what it is. There is but one way out for you. You better take it before your filthy, abnormal, fraudulent self is bared to the nation.

To Harold Ross, editor of the New Yorker, *from Alexander Woollcott, after Ross had forgotten a dinner engagement*

I agree with you that the fewer dealings one has with you and the fewer debts one permits you to incur, the less chance there is to be subjected to your discourtesy. I have enjoyed your company so much that I have been one of the last to make this simple discovery. The remedy is even simpler.

It seems hard to believe that you really think I objected to your breaking a dinner engagement with me.

As I was sound asleep upstairs, I didn't even know you hadn't come. I *was* a trifle revolted that you should have thought your casual imposition on the amiable Junior so richly comic. And your subsequent paroxysms of mirth made me a little sick. Any tyro in psychology recognizes that urchin defense mechanism, but the person who jeers at me when there is a good audience and waits for privacy to apologize is manifesting a kind of poltroonery I find hard to deal with.

Hawley tells me that the money for my fourth of the house equipment is due from you. You will remember that we agreed to leave the fixing of the amount to him. He has, I believe, figured this out. Then you were to take over, I believe, some proportion of the $325 I spent on my apartment. Will you send me a check for this or your note for three months? I should be reluctant to burden you with more favorable terms. You can, if need be, borrow the money from some innocent who does not suspect how deeply he will thereby be incurring your antipathy.

I think your slogan "Liberty or Death" is splendid and whichever one you finally decide upon will be all right with me.

To his enemies in the medical profession, living and dead, from Theophrastus Bombastus von Hohenheim (Paracelsus), the sixteenth-century German physician and chemist

You shall follow me, you Avicenna, Galen, you gentlemen of Paris, Montpellier, Germany, Belgium and Vienna. . . . None shall stay in a corner and have the dogs piss at him—all shall follow me, and the monarchy of medicine shall be mine. This dirt you shall eat! All the universities and all the old writers put together are less talented than my asshole.

To Dr. Zev Wanderer, a behavioral therapist in Los Angeles, from a patient he had been treating for pathological shyness, after Dr. Wanderer had sent her a note indicating his concern over her failure to show up for several consecutive group sessions

You have your nerve, expecting me to drive all the way from Torrance to come to one of your assertion training groups. Do you think your time is more valuable than mine? I have started my own assertion training group and now I am leading people here in Torrance.

To a suitor, 1834, from a lady who viewed without enthusiasm the gentleman's proposal of marriage

After the decided disapprobation I have constantly evinced to your attentions, I was rather surprised at receiving an offer of marriage from you.

I am sorry that you have thus placed me under the disagreeable necessity of speaking on a subject so repugnant to my feelings; but candour and truth compel me to return an instant and positive negative to your proposal.

I trust, therefore, you will no longer persist in disturbing, by such unavailing efforts, the peace of, sir, your obedient servant.

To an inmate at Attica prison, New York, who, hoping to borrow money for an appeal, had answered an advertisement placed by a man claiming to want to "share his inheritance with a woman," and who subsequently terminated the ensuing correspondence upon being asked to guarantee the granting of his wife's sexual favors in return for a loan

I received your final letter and want to reply.

I placed an ad *specifically* asking for a *woman* but when you wrote to me I treated you decently and took the time to try to help you if I could. When I asked your help in return, your answer is a complete no without a word mentioning how my proposition will affect me, just that it offends *your* self-respect.

You're a creep just like I always thought you were. You want me to *give* you hundreds of dollars and when

I ask for something that *you* have to give up something for, you refuse. You're such a friend that when you can't get money from me, you discard me completely like a piece of shit. You said you had 2 things to offer, "friendship and sincerity," where are they now that you haven't been able to con me into letting you use me?

You say what better use of my money than to find someone deserving of sharing it, you're deserving only of my hate and contempt. I have a few friends in the prison system who may pay you a visit (strictly social and nothing illegal or violent of course since who would be foolish enough to put a threat in writing).

So rot in your cell like you deserve and keep whatever self-respect you can claim to have while you're punished and suffering 24 hours a day. You've sacrificed your freedom for your love of women who will turn on you sooner or later like all bitches do. Just think how you could be *free* lying on the beach in luxury rather than sweating in a prison cell for years. No out of state pen pals is worth the hell you are going to endure every day as the result of your idiotic decision not to cooperate with me.

I could say a lot more but I'm going out to enjoy life instead of wasting time on a loser like you.

P.S. I hope you get gang-raped and crippled tonight, filthy scumbag!

To a gentleman who had complained, in forceful fashion, about the quality of the accommodation in a London hotel, from the hotel's manager

I have received your letter, and I must tell you that we consider your accusations to be unfounded. After hearing from you, we conducted a thorough examination of the room you occupied. There were no cockroaches or spiders in the room, as you allege, only bedbugs. This was due to heavy traffic from the Middle East during the summer months. Many hotels in London suffer from this same problem. It's not our fault. I suggest you try another hotel next time and see what happens.

To John Kendrick Bangs, a nineteenth-century American humorist and speechwriter, from an important industrialist, after Bangs had charitably offered to write a speech for the industrialist on more generous terms than he charged the equally important Chauncey Depew

(VIA WESTERN UNION)

YOUR LETTER JUST RECEIVED. IF CHAUNCEY DEPEW'S SPEECHES ARE WRITTEN BY YOU THEN I DON'T WANT ONE.

To anyone whose peace of mind one wishes to disturb: two old standards from Anon.

This is to inform you that your application for membership in Schizophrenics Anonymous has been rejected. The S.A. has decided that, despite your frequent screaming and attempts to attack mailboxes, you don't fulfill all of our membership qualifications.

However, by now you must realize that you are being watched. If this becomes increasingly upsetting to you, you might consider applying for membership in the Society of Paranoiacs. But don't be surprised if the S.P. doesn't respond immediately. After all, they may be nervous admitting someone as weird as you.

Perhaps you have heard of me and my nationwide campaign in the cause of temperance. Each year for the past fourteen years, I have made a tour of the country and delivered lectures on the evils of DRINKING.

On these tours I have been accompanied by my young friend and assistant, Philip Lindstrom. Philip was a pathetic case: a young man of good family and excellent background whose life had been ruined by excessive indulgence in whiskey, rum, and beer. Philip would appear with me at my lectures and sit on the platform babbling incoherently and staring at the audience through bloodshot eyes, while I would point him out as an example of what DRINKING can do.

Last month, unfortunately, poor Philip died. A

mutual friend told me about you and gave me your name, so I am wondering if you would be free to accompany me on this year's tour and take Philip's place. I will gladly send you the schedule.

To George Washington, from Tom Paine

As to you, sir, treacherous in private friendship, and a hypocrite in public life, the world will be puzzled to decide whether you are an impostate or an imposter; whether you have abandoned good principles, or whether you ever had any.

To a lady who had written calling then-Governor Jimmy Carter of Georgia a "gutless peanut brain" because he had not protested against the busing of schoolchildren to achieve racial integration, from Jody Powell, press secretary to the governor

Among the many burdens that fall upon a governor, one of the most exasperating is having to read barely legible letters from morons like you.

I am very happy that I can at least spare the governor from having to respond. I respectfully suggest that you take two running jumps and go straight to hell.

To a constituent of Representative Max Baucus of Wisconsin, who had written in opposition to the congressman's support of mandatory participation in the Social Security System, from an assistant to the congressman

The IRS people are very nice. They allow every representative to send in the names of 20 people and then they audit these people. You see, the people at IRS understand that we get a lot of ridiculous letters from our constituents and want to help us get a few of them off our backs, so to speak.

One of my staff saw your letter and figured you were a real crackpot. What can I say except that I'm sorry? I figured I'd warn you so you could get your files in order.

To a constituent of Representative David R. Obey of Wisconsin, who had accused the congressman of persecuting witnesses in the course of a congressional committee hearing, from an assistant to the congressman

Couldn't help but get a chuckle out of your letter. We are so pleased to know that you have enough self-confidence to establish yourself as a self-appointed censurer. Of course, nobody has yet communicated to this office in any way the sense of being misused, but we are nevertheless always so pleased when a man of such obvious importance seeks to protect poor gentlemen from a big, bad Congressman.

You know, every so often we get a letter so pompous that it reminds one of the old poem "warty bliggens."

i met a toad
the other day by the name
of warty bliggens
he was sitting under
a toadstool
feeling contented
he explained that when the cosmos
was created
that toadstool was especially
planned for his personal
shelter from sun and rain
thought out and prepared
for him

do not tell me
said warty bliggens
that there is not a purpose
in the universe
the thought is blasphemy

a little more
conversation revealed

that warty bliggens
considers himself to be
the center of the said
universe
the earth exists
to grow toadstools for him
to sit under
the sun to give him light
by day and the moon
and wheeling constellations
to make beautiful
the night for the sake of
warty bliggens

to what act of yours
do you impute
this interest on the part
of the creator
of the universe
i asked him
why is that you
are so greatly favored

ask rather
said warty bliggens
what the universe
has done to deserve me
if i were a
human being i would
not laugh
too complacently
at poor warty bliggens
for similar
absurdities

have only too often
lodged in the crinkles
of the human cerebrum

We hope you can keep your partisan zeal under somewhat better control than you have shown on numerous instances in the past until you receive a copy of the committee hearings which are not yet printed. They will speak for themselves and we are frankly much more interested in what the record shows than in what can be found in the mind of a partisan zealot.

To a lady in Massachusetts who had written criticizing the position of Senator James B. Allen of Alabama regarding the Panama Canal treaties, from an assistant to the senator

I'm writing to advise you that your letter has been received and put in Senator Allen's crackpot file. There are quite a few letters from Massachusetts in this file. Evidently your state is a melting pot for neurotics, cranks, and other individuals with sub-normal mentalities.

To a lady who had written to Senator Stephen M. Young of Ohio calling him, among other things, "an old reprobate," from Senator Young

Lady, reading your abusive, insulting and untruthful letter causes me to feel happy I am not your husband.

To a lady who had sent a letter to the Cincinnati Enquirer *accusing Senator Young of "smearing" the John Birch Society, from the senator*

In the interest of fairness, I feel it my duty to send this letter, which was clipped from the *Enquirer*, to you and let you know that some crackbrain is using your name for such correspondence. Possibly you will wish to see that adequate measures are taken to protect your good name.

To a gentleman who had become extremely agitated upon hearing that a horse had been flown from Pakistan to Mrs. John F. Kennedy by the U.S. Air Force, and who thereupon demanded that Senator Young send him a horse "in the same manner," from the senator

Acknowledging your letter wherein you insult the wife of our President, I am wondering why you need a horse when there is already one jackass at your address.

To artist Lowell Darling, after he had written to Mayor Abe Beame of New York proposing, as a cure for the troubled city, the application of giant needles, from the mayor's press secretary

The Mayor has received your letter concerning acupuncture for the City of New York and has asked me to reply for him.

If your suggestion is intended to needle the people of our City, we get the point.

To the poet Jonathan Williams, from Governor Lester Maddox of Georgia, after Mr. Williams had written to the Governor asking if he would be good enough to specify publicly that his statements on racial matters reflected only his own feelings on the subject and not those of all Southerners

THE SAME TO YOU!

To the manager of a traveling theatrical company, from Mark Twain, after the gentleman had informed Twain that he had "taken the liberty" of dramatizing Tom Sawyer *and wanted permission to use Twain's name as the author of the play*

And so it has got around to you, at last; and you have "taken the liberty." You are No. 1365. When 1364 sweeter and better people, including the author, have tried to dramatize Tom Sawyer and did not arrive, what sort of show do you suppose you stand? That is a book, dear sir, which cannot be dramatized. One might as well try to dramatize any other hymn. Tom Sawyer is simply a hymn, put into prose form to give it a worldly air.

Why the pale doubt that flitteth dim and nebulous athwart the forecastle of your third sentence? Have no fears. Your piece will be a Go. It will go out the back door on the first night. They've all done it—the 1364. So will—1365. Not one of us ever thought of the simple device of half-soling himself with a stove lid. Ah, what suffering a little hindsight would have saved us. Treasure this hint.

How kind of you to invite me to the funeral. Go to; I have attended a thousand of them. I have seen Tom Sawyer's remains in all the different kinds of dramatic shrouds there are. You cannot start anything fresh. Are you serious when you propose to pay my expence—if that is the Susquehannian way of spelling it? And can you be aware that I charge a hundred dollars a mile when I travel for pleasure? Do you realize that it is 432 miles to Susquehanna? Would it be handy for you to send me the $43,200 first, so I could be counting it as I come along; because railroading is pretty dreary to a sensitive nature when there's nothing sordid to buck at for Zeitvertreib.

Now as I understand it, dear and magnanimous 1365, you are going to re-create Tom Sawyer dramatically, and then do me the compliment to put me in the bills as father of this shady offspring. Sir, do you know that this kind of compliment has destroyed people before now? Listen.

Twenty-four years ago, I was strangely handsome. The remains of it are still visible through the rifts of time. I was so handsome that human activities ceased as if spellbound when I came in view, and even inanimate things stopped to look—like locomotives, and district messenger boys and so on. In San Francisco, in rainy season I was often mistaken for fair weather. Upon one occasion I was traveling in the Sonora region, and stopped for an hour's nooning, to rest my horse and myself. All the town came out to look. A Piute squaw named her baby for me—a voluntary compliment which pleased me greatly.

Other attentions were paid me. Last of all arrived the president and faculty of Sonora University and offered me the post of Professor of Moral Culture and Dogmatic Humanities; which I accepted gratefully, and entered at once upon my duties. But my name had pleased the Indians, and in the deadly kindness of their hearts they went on naming their babies after me. I tried to stop it, but the Indians could not understand why I should object to so manifest a compliment. The thing grew and grew and spread and spread and became exceedingly embarrassing. The University stood it a couple of years; but then for the sake of the college they felt obliged to call a halt, although I had the sympathy of the whole faculty.

The president himself said to me, "I am as sorry as I can be for you, and would still hold out if there were any hope ahead; but you see how it is: there are a hundred and thirty-two of them already, and fourteen precincts to hear from. The circumstance has brought your name into most wide and unfortunate renown. It causes much comment—I believe that that is not an overstatement. Some of this comment is palliative, but some of it—by patrons at a distance, who only know the statistics without the explanation—is offensive, and in some cases even violent. Nine students have been called home. The trustees of the college have been growing more and more uneasy all these last months—steadily along with the implacable increase in your census—and I will not conceal from you that more than once they have touched upon the expediency of a change in the Professorship of Moral Culture. The coarsely sarcastic editorial in yesterday's Alta—headed Give the Moral Acrobat a Rest—has brought things to a crisis, and I am charged with the unpleasant duty of receiving your resignation."

I know you only mean me a kindness, dear 1365, but it is a most deadly mistake. Please do not name your Injun for me.

To anyone who approached him with a tiresome request, from the author and critic Edmund Wilson

EDMUND WILSON REGRETS THAT IT IS IMPOSSIBLE FOR HIM TO:
READ MANUSCRIPTS,
WRITE ARTICLES OR BOOKS TO ORDER,
WRITE FOREWORDS OR INTRODUCTIONS,
MAKE STATEMENTS FOR PUBLICITY PURPOSES,
DO ANY KIND OF EDITORIAL WORK,
JUDGE LITERARY CONTESTS,
GIVE INTERVIEWS,
CONDUCT EDUCATIONAL COURSES,
DELIVER LECTURES,
GIVE TALKS OR MAKE SPEECHES,
BROADCAST OR APPEAR ON TELEVISION,
TAKE PART IN WRITERS' CONGRESSES,
ANSWER QUESTIONNAIRES,
CONTRIBUTE TO OR TAKE PART IN SYMPOSIUMS OR "PANELS" OF ANY KIND,
CONTRIBUTE MANUSCRIPTS FOR SALES,
DONATE COPIES OF HIS BOOKS TO LIBRARIES,
ALLOW HIS NAME TO BE USED ON LETTERHEADS,
SUPPLY PERSONAL INFORMATION ABOUT HIMSELF,
SUPPLY PHOTOGRAPHS OF HIMSELF,
SUPPLY OPINIONS ON LITERARY OR OTHER SUBJECTS.

Finally, perhaps the most famous hate letter of all time, celebrated equally for its succinctness and for the elegant scatology of its message: to a gentleman who had written impudently, from Voltaire

I am seated in the smallest room in the house. I have your letter before me. Soon it will be behind me.